Soul Sampler

Elizabeth Hahn

2010

From one emeritus to another, congratulations!

Soul

Sampler

Elizabeth

RedLine Books
White Bluff, Tennessee
2004

The author and publisher wish to thank the copyright holders for permission to quote from the following poems:

Czeslaw Milosz, "Faith," trans. Robert Hass, Robert Pinsky, and Renata Gorczynski; Rainer Maria Rilke, "A Walk," trans. Robert Bly; Rumi, "Say Yes Quickly," trans. Coleman Barks and John Moyne, all in *The Rag and Bone Shop of the Heart: Poems for Men*, ed. Robert Bly, James Hillman, and Michael Meade (HarperCollins, 1992). Wendell Berry, "The Current," "The Hidden Singer," and "The Slip," in *The Selected Poems of Wendell Berry* (Perseus Book Group, 1998); Bill Brown, "October Poem," in *The Gods of Little Pleasures* (Sow's Ear Press, 2001); Joy Harjo, "Prayer," in *The Woman That Fell from the Sky* (W. W. Norton, 1994); Jane Kenyon, "Briefly It Enters, and Briefly Speaks" (© 1996 by the Estate of Jane Kenyon; rpt. from *Otherwise: New and Selected Poems* [Saint Paul: Graywolf]); Maxine Kumin, "Seeing the Bones," in *Selected Poems, 1960–1990* (W. W. Norton, 1997); Philip Levine, "Making It New" and "Silent in America," in *New Selected Poems* (Knopf, 1994); Mary Oliver, "The Journey," in *Dream Work* (Atlantic Monthly Press, 1986) and "When Death Comes," in *New and Selected Poems* (Beacon, 1992); Naomi Replansky, "Housing Shortage," in *Ring Song: Poems* (Scribner, 1952); Pattiann Rogers, "The Family Is All There Is," in *Splitting and Binding* (Wesleyan University [Conn.] Press, 1992); Rumi, "Name," trans. Robert Bly, in *When Grapes Turn to Wine* (Yellow Moon, 1983); Jeffrey Skinner, "Problems," in *A Guide to Forgetting* (Graywolf, 1988); John Smelcer, "Ascension," in *Riversongs* (Poetics, Inc. 2001); Wislawa Szymborska, "Conversation with a Stone," in *View With A Grain of Sand* (Harcourt Brace & Co., 1993); William Carlos Williams, "Danse Russe," in *The Collected Poems of William Carlos Williams: 1909-1939*, vol. I (New Directions, 1968); Baron Wormser, "Poem of the American Senior Citizenry," in *When* (Sarabande Books, 1997) and "Atoms," in *Atoms, Soul Music and Other Poems* (Latham, N.Y.: British American Publishing: Paris Review Editions, 1989).

Manufactured in the United States of America by
RedLine Books
2280 Jones Creek Rd.
White Bluff, Tennessee
(615) 797 3043
redlinebooks@bardyoung.com

"Who goes to dine must take his feast
Or find the banquet mean
The table is not laid without
Till it is laid within. . . . "
— Emily Dickinson

Contents

Preface   ix

3	Awe	Nurture	51
7	Becoming	Overdoing	54
11	Community	Practices	57
15	Despair	Quiet	61
18	Ecstasy	Resourcefulness	64
23	Forgiveness	Soul	68
27	Gifts	Time	72
31	Hospitality	Understanding	76
34	Independence	Valuing	79
38	Joy	Word	83
41	Kin	X	86
44	Location	Yes	89
47	Mourning	Zone	93

A Selection of Prayers and Meditations   97

Notes on Sources   105

Blank pages for reader's notes   110

Preface

To begin with a sampler, a piece of cloth embroidered with the alphabet and attractive designs, used to serve as a young girl's needlework primer. Working from A-Z, the novice slowly mastered the art of the needle.

In the same way, I decided to move from A-Z in this book, exploring what I have been learning about our souls. Often, like all beginners, I needed to go back and start over again, as I searched for ways to build a spirit-filled life.

Have you noticed that while we constantly feed our minds and bodies, our souls often go hungry? Why would we neglect the most important part of our being? Maybe we have not yet acknowledged that the soul is our center point.

Besides being a piece of needlework, a sampler is also a collection of morsels—small bits that invite us to try something new. Whether you are a life-time believer in the power of the soul or a new adventurer in the world of the spirit, I hope these small pieces will awaken your appetite.

In the beginning I thought this book would grow out of quiet periods set aside from my usually busy life. That, after all, was what I wanted to share—the importance of "inviting one's soul," of making time and space to recognize and nurture our souls. But a book instructs its author. All my writing turned out to be rooted in the day-to-day contacts, commitments, and activities I felt I needed to set aside. The understandings I thought would spring from solitude turned out to be deeply communal.

Even the progression of the various chapters, so logically following the alphabet, resisted my initial intentions. Thoughts about "Time" occurred to me before ideas about "Hospitality"; I knew more about Joy than Despair. The result of all this unpredictability is that you, the reader, can, if you prefer, progress from the front cover to the back, or you can read chapters as they appeal to you, as your interests of the moment dictate, as the need arises. The thread that holds the sampler together is the recognition that each of us possesses a unique and eternal soul. To explore together how we will honor and nurture our souls is the most important endeavor I know.

I also wanted to provide some blank pages for your personal thoughts, questions, and reactions as you were reading. Further, even though every bookstore provides us with a vast array of prayers and meditations, several are offered here, from a variety of traditions and epochs, simply because through the years they have spoken movingly to me. May they move you, too.

So many people have helped with this book it would be impossible to name them all. But there is another way to recognize them, and that is by place. All my life I seem to have been blessed by coming down "where I ought to be," as the Shaker hymn puts it. How many other twelve-year-olds find themselves in the grammar school in Clinton, Connecticut, playing the daily hymn on a pump-organ? And even learn to like it?

And within a year, accompanied by my sister, I came down again, to learn the strict routines of a remote boarding school. Yes, it was strict living, but somehow it all worked; I was "where I ought to be." The Northfield Mount Hermon School proved to be a guardian of our spirits as well as our minds. Our teachers and ministers provided rich fare for our morning "quiet time," daily chapel, evening prayers. Their books and pictures still grace my office shelves, giving me insights all these years later.

After awhile, even the truly difficult times seemed to evolve into something understandable, that "ought to be" feeling. For instance, my early marriage—our beautiful healthy son born while I was still in college, and then my husband's being recalled into military service—had at the outset all the marks of upheaval. But the places that were soon made for us all made sense. Grandmothers and grandfathers, even a great grandfather, adjusted their lives and living space, took us in, held us close. "No place like home"? Only the vagrant understands.

Other places nourished and taught us: in Milford, Connecticut, the nursery school where our next son was so warmly welcomed, and where I learned about teaching and learning; Milford's First Congregational Church where lifelong friendships developed through diverse study groups, retreats, and active community life; later, the neighboring Orange Congregational Church, and the Guilford Congregational Church, each one slightly different, each one identical in generosity, commitment to social justice, and individual affirmation.

So, when we moved to Nashville, it was no surprise to find that Brookmeade Congregational Church was a close kin of our New England church family. Here were the same marks of devotion: a modestly small building with simple furnishings, an active congregation marked by people in the helping professions, a generosity of spirit that shows itself in outreach, counseling, benevolences, celebrations of the Spirit. So many Brookmeaders, men and women, even the children I have learned from in church school, reside in these pages. Over almost twenty years, their gifts to me are impossible to count; they live between the lines in the oral histories we have collected and in the prolific margin notes of books we have studied; they show themselves in drawings and photographs on the walls of the Sunday school and, most of all, in the embrace of our church family. I can see you all, and I thank you. I must also express my thanks to Sherrye and Bard Young of RedLine Books, for their excellent editorial and book-designing skills. I owe so much to them for the accuracy of the text and for the wonderful look of this little book.

The workplace, too, is hospitable. Sometimes, at the *Cumberland Poetry Review,* sometimes at Filmhouse, our son's film production company in Nashville, bright and energetic people contribute to our thinking. Local writing groups also provide a forum for current work.

I must mention one more hallowed place: when you can, go to Franconia, New Hampshire. Trudge up the dirt road to the Frost Place—on your left, the Presidential Range and Cannon Mountain, on your right Robert Frost's weathered dairy barn, where poets from across the country gather to share their work. The leaders have guided these conferences and festivals for the last twenty-two years. They have the most cultivated hearts alive. Feel the Spirit.

Soul Sampler

we

That sudden overwhelming feeling of reverence and wonder! Have you experienced it lately? The truth is, most of us have not.

We hear ourselves saying, "Oh, that's awful!" in response to someone's misfortune, or we may exclaim, "Awesome!" as someone describes an impressive feat. But suddenly to be swept up in an irresistible surge of wonder, delight, even fear—to experience awe—is pretty rare these days.

We could blame our lack of awe on the pace of our lives, saying as the poet Jeffrey Skinner does in "Problems":

> God is transient,
> and though He wants badly for us to see through
> His disguise, placing Himself constantly before us
> in the course of every ordinary day, we are busy,
> very, very busy. What an effort it takes to love!
> So much of the self in the way, like a building
> that must be blasted to make the horizon visible.[1]

Or we could point out that awe-inspiring, mountaintop experiences are hard to come by, immersed as we are in work down here on the plains. And that is so often true.

But as we stop to think, we realize that our lives, even those that may seem entirely ordinary on the surface, do indeed hold moments of awe. That surge of wonder and excitement may come as we step into some completely new place, whether at the edge of a vast canyon or in the warm, turquoise waters off a southern island. Awe may overcome us as we enter a cathedral, a small rustic church, a museum. Sometimes we feel that spine-tingling sensation as we hear the first notes of a long-awaited concert.

Suddenly we are swept up into something larger, whether the grandeur of nature or the thrill of human achievement. As Robert Bly translates Rilke's "A Walk,"

> We are grasped by what we cannot grasp;
> it has its inner light, even from a distance—
> and changes us, even if we do not reach it,
> into something else, which, hardly sensing it, we already are.[2]

That interplay between the invisible with "its inner light" and us, the visible, is what we recognize as our souls stirring.

Besides the awe-filled moments we treasure from our past, there are new and compelling developments that evoke wonder. In this unique period in the history of the universe, we are receiving fascinating new information, from geologists, astronomers, physicists, microbiologists. We discover we are part of an emerging universe with startlingly common elements.

In an unprecedented flood of empirical data, as the scholar and theologian

Awe ~ BCDEFGHIJKLMNOPQRSTUVWXYZ~

Thomas Berry points out, we are now "listening to the earth tell its story through the signals that it sends to us from outer space, through the light that comes to us from the stars, through the geological formations of the earth and through a vast number of other evidences." Not only are we learning about the grandeur and magnitude of the cosmos, we are claiming our rightful role as an integral part of it. "We participate in its life. We are nourished, instructed and healed by this community. In and through this community we enter into communion with that numinous mystery on which all things depend for their existence and activity."[3] We hear Thomas's conviction in the worshipful words of the Hebrew psalmist, "Our God, in whom we live and move and have our being."

Is this knowledge of the common sacred makeup of all creation damaging to the faith some of us grew up with?

It need not be. The greatest religious leaders have told us for years, "Your god is too small. Your churches, too small." Perhaps our very souls are too small.

Now we begin to feel that physical prickle of awe—that arresting realization that we are part of an enormously creative, ongoing "journey of the universe." From the beginning of the galaxies to the formation of the earth, the development of life, you and I have been a part of the process. Place yourself within that context, an integral part of the creative, ongoing, sacred journey— the stuff of awe!

But if thoughts of the magnitude of galaxies seem overwhelming, another kind of knowledge is even more awe inspiring. It is the fact of our own sacred nature. Beneath all our outer varieties of race, creed, and clan, we are one in our inner makeup. We each have a soul.

Nimble minds, courageous hearts, constantly self-restoring bodies—these are what we present to the world. They are our vehicles. But all our traveling will be in circles unless we accept the soul as driver.

And what steers the soul? The ministers Harold Freer and Francis Hall remind us, "We must begin by believing God is interested in each one of us, and by living in accordance with that belief."[4]

Now we feel the surge of awe, the realization that we are not isolated creatures, no matter how productive or "successful" our lives appear to be. Rather, our lives exist within an ongoing sacred process in which each of us is known and loved by God. It is that certainty that inspires our deepest awe.

ecoming

Nothing stands still. From the farthest reaches of the universe to the ground under our feet, all is in motion. Even the hardest substances we know are energy fields teeming with atomic movement.

Surrounded by all that activity, it's interesting how uncomfortable we feel with the idea of movement or change. Rather, we pride ourselves on being "finished with something," of having "gotten things under control," as though life could be predictably managed.

Perhaps because we are so good at making "finished" products, we have grown uncomfortable with "unfinished business" or "loose ends." We complete courses, satisfy requirements, meet the deadline, ship the product. We want things accomplished, taken care of. No wonder we resist the notion of ourselves or our lives in a state of becoming. "Becoming what?" we ask.

In some wealthy social circles, young women are still sent to "finishing schools," before being formally presented to society. An interesting paradox: To become an acceptable product in the courtship and marriage arena, a girl has to be "made presentable." She needs to be groomed and polished. (Does this sound like a horse or dog show?)

So the young woman, the outward "product," becomes immensely alluring and refined, well versed in all the social graces. But let's think a moment about the inner process. Schooled in ways to please others, what does she learn about pleasing herself? If her worth depends on others' approval, what does she assume about her own value as a mature person? Where is the inner grace, a sense of wholeness and infinite value? Unfortunately, the "Cinderella complex" has never been limited to the wealthy.

Let's examine, for a minute, our ideas about our spiritual makeup. No one doubts the powerful reality of our emotions, our minds, our bodies, but when someone mentions the reality of our souls, we begin to fidget. "Uh, oh," the listener objects, "Let's not get too heavy." Or, "I'm not big into religion," the teenager will reply. Nervously.

Religion, however, concerns the outward expression of belief. What we want to explore is the inward expression. We want to come to know that part of each human being that outlives time and space, the part that is of final value, that is sacred. Why is it sacred? Because, no matter what religion or belief system we embrace, we carry within us the essential element of humanity—a soul.

If you doubt that, consider the people who have been stripped of all their human attributes, whether through overwhelming illness, catastrophe, or simply by age. Whether in a crippled body or on a death bed, their remaining life, their vital principle, can still be felt, is attested to, time and again. It is their soul.

I have an Alaskan Indian friend, John Smelcer, who tells of the reality of the souls of animals. There is no doubt in his, and his tribe's, mind that the earth contains the spirits both of ancestors and animals. Yes, they have, in the slang expression, "gone to the happy hunting grounds." But their spirits frequently reappear—the moose vaguely seen on the other side of the frozen lake, the caribou who leaves no tracks in the crusted snow.

Here is the connection: Whether you personally believe in the ongoing spirits of animals and other life is not the issue. The truth is that what makes us human, the very essence of our being, is that spark of the divine, our soul.

Agnostics are quick to point out that what unites us is our mortality. What they fail to see is that what unites us further is our divinity. No matter what name you call the godhead, or whether you have never given it much thought, our souls recognize their maker.

We feel the stirrings of our souls in all kinds of times and places: in settings of great natural beauty, in moments of supreme joy, in fellowship and in solitude, in grief and in pain. We cry out in gratitude when something wonderful happens. "Hallelujah!" we shout. We may cry out in despair and anguish when life seems unbearable. Our souls have a powerful voice.

Then let us not carelessly ignore the most important messages we could receive! Such active ignorance is an overt denial of our shared humanity Rather, to achieve the kind of balance we seek—in body, emotions, mind, and soul—we need to find times and places where we can simply "invite our souls."

We will begin by setting aside a daily time, even as short as ten or fifteen minutes, to center ourselves. These quiet periods allow us to shed our usual "defenses," our learned ways of putting aside uncomfortable thoughts, unwelcome emotions. We will learn to accept ourselves, acknowledging that we often carry within us anger, jealousy, grief, remorse, even fear. We come to see, as the psychologist James Hillman puts it, that "character is characters; our nature is a plural complexity."[1] And through that wonderful insight we will come to recognize, to know, and to accept the "different" parts of ourselves.

So, at the outset, we need these quiet times to develop self-awareness and self-acceptance. Out of healthy self-love will spring the love for our Creator and others.

As our daily practice continues and we increasingly open our lives to our Creator, our silences will become listening and speaking. We will feel, increasingly, the desire to give thanks, to praise, to ask for what we need.

We have been exploring the idea of "becoming": to come into being, to develop. Contrary to the expectations of our culture, we are not "finished products," not fully mature. But by purposefully turning our attention to the most vital part of our nature, we will allow our souls room and time to develop. We will help them to come into their rightful being.

Over a century ago, Walt Whitman described the persistence of "a noiseless, patient spider," as it constantly spins its sticky thread from the center of its body. He likened it to the work of the soul:

> And you O my soul where you stand.
> Surrounded, detached, in measureless oceans of space,
> Ceaselessly musing, venturing,
> Throwing, seeking the spheres to connect them,
> Till the bridge you will need be form'd, till the ductile anchor hold,
> Till the gossamer thread you fling catch somewhere, O, my soul.

The bridge will be formed, the anchor will hold, if we allow it to happen.

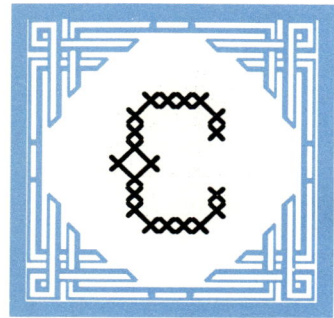# ommunity

Such a familiar word. We say, "Our friends moved to another community," or "Ridge Top is such an outstanding community," and we usually think of a group of similar people who have chosen to live in the same area. Why do people make that kind of choice?

Often, they want to place their children in "better" schools. Or perhaps they want to place themselves in a more "secure" home. But clearly, the desire to live in what may even be called a "gated community" is based less on which people are allowed in than on which people are kept out.

In this kind of community, the word *neighbor* has taken on a bland sameness. Whereas the original Greek phrase meaning "a stranger at the gates" was used to insure that any traveler, friend or foe, was to be given food and shelter, the same phrase now stirs images of someone threatening or undesirable. When we recall that the Latin root of *community* is *communis*, meaning "common possession or participation," we see how radically most modern societies have changed. What was once inclusive is now often determinedly exclusive.

Clearly, the challenge of building human community is more complex than the matter of simply examining where we choose to live. Thanks to the magic of communications satellites, global positioning systems, and the Internet, we are suddenly swept up into places and situations we never imagined seeing or knowing. This can be thrilling—the prospect of vast connections to an ever-widening array of human contacts; or it can be tremendously disturbing—the sudden awareness of others' suffering, their oppression, poverty, disease. The quality of life we take for granted suddenly seems distorted, out of proportion. Or we may come to feel that the differences among cultures may seem so dividing that we will never "come together."

Perhaps we can find hope in recent endeavors like the Nashville-based Seeds Project. Teams of writers, photographers, radio journalists, musicians, artists, and video and television crews are setting out to document the activities of UN and nongovernmental organizations in their humanitarian work around the world.

The Seeds Project will produce books, films, multimedia exhibits, concerts, and other events that will transcend cultural boundaries by putting the reader, viewer, listener "in the shoes" of the aid workers, the combatants, and especially the survivors, caught in global crisis. The stories may be about "land mines in Cambodia, family separation in Rwanda, or the plight of women and children in countries worldwide."[1] The hope is that sharing such "real life" experience will encourage dialogue not only among agencies but within concerned groups everywhere.

Certainly, until basic human needs are met, long-term humanitarian aid cannot succeed. But in the challenge to live responsibly within community, endeavors like the Seeds Project enlarge our thinking and feeling.

Our new, heightened knowledge of people around the world is often intensely painful. It evokes not only shock and fear but also pity, as we grasp how closely we are all connected, all part of a vast community. Some people, unaccustomed to graphic television or newspaper images of war and suffering, try to steel themselves against sympathy. They close their souls as well as their minds.

Shortly before her untimely death, a sensitive Nashville teenager voiced her despair over our failure to honor our common humanity. Ellen Bell wrote in her poem "Everyman,"

> Everyman is one and the same.
> But everyman has one man
> To call strange,
> For he is so blind
> He can see only the skin's color,
> For he is so deaf
> He hears only the tongue's strange roll,
> For he is so narrow
> He chastises a foreign tenet,
> And all the while he fails
> To feel the prevailing human spirit.[2]

As a testament to "the prevailing human spirit," the renowned photographer Edward Steichen assembled an exhibition of photographs for the New York's Museum of Modern Art. The exhibit, compiled over fifty years ago and later published as a book, was called "The Family of Man." From tens of thousands of pictures, Steichen selected 503 photos from 68 countries, pictures he felt caught, better than words could ever do, "the essential oneness of man." It is one of the most compelling collections you can imagine.

As Carl Sandburg described it,

Everywhere is love and love making, weddings and babies from generation to generation keeping The Family of Man alive and continuing. Everywhere the sun, moon and stars, the climates and weathers, have meanings for people. Though meanings vary, we are alike in all countries and tribes in trying to read what sky, land and sea say to us. Alike and ever alike, we are on all continents in the need of love, food, clothing, work, speech, worship, sleep, games, dancing, fun. From tropics to arctics, humanity lives with these needs so alike, so inexorably alike.[3]

Not only are our needs astonishingly alike. Our very makeup is proving to be amazingly similar, as microbiologists unravel the secrets of RNA codes. Provided with insights from 3.5 billion years ago, scientists are discovering that virtually all living organisms are derived from the same fossil blueprint. The genetic makeup of plants, it turns out, is stunningly similar to that of animals.

Talk about a community!

 **espair**

In Bunyan's *Pilgrim's Progress*, the hero must undergo a series of tests before arriving at the Heavenly City. One of the worst of these is being mired in the Slough of Despond. A slough? It's just not one of those everyday words. Perhaps it had something to do with pigs?

Even if we can imagine such a quagmire, we are pretty sure we have not sunk that low. And yet all of us have experienced that deep sense of hopelessness that will not respond to reason.

Today, therapists tell us despair springs from many sources. We may be carrying old wounds from childhood, unresolved angers and griefs that were never brought into the open for healing. We may be carrying the seeds of constant self-doubt or self-criticism sown by a perfectionist teacher or parent. Possibly, we may never have acknowledged, and been able to overcome, an innate sense of yearning or loneliness.

But even those who are normally "in good spirits" may be overcome by a deep sense of despair. Beneath their customary optimism lies a sensitivity to the world around them, its injustices, its suffering. Often these deeply thoughtful, contemplative people foresee all too easily the long-term effects of human greed and exploitation.

In the 1940s, nuclear scientists watched a peculiarly shaped cloud rise above a desert plain in the remote American Southwest, signaling the creation of the first atomic explosion. One can imagine those physicists joyful, even jubilant, to have completed a seemingly impossible undertaking assigned them by their government. Instead, several have told us they experienced a deep sense of foreboding, even grief, as they sensed the consequences of such power. They could foresee, with horrifying clarity, the military uses of their success, the inevitable cost in human lives.

Surely, one of the gifts God has given us is this sort of spiritual imagination. It manifests itself in our heightened awareness, both in very personal contacts and in a more far-reaching concern over the world around us. We find ourselves deeply touched by reports of human suffering. At the same time that we become more sensitive to others' needs, we find ourselves increasingly vulnerable. The newspaper image of a child's face, quieted in death, can haunt us.

When despair over human suffering sweeps over us, let it come. Accept the weight of it. Do not at that moment expect to change anything. What this acceptance means is not that we are overwhelmed by it, but that we enter it and bear it with others. We learn through the spirit what it is like for all those who grieve, who suffer, are displaced, dispossessed. We remember that, throughout history, people have been driven from their homes, sent on forced marches, sold into slavery. Through such empathy we allow ourselves to become deeply, caringly human.

After we have deliberately exposed ourselves to despair, have accepted its crushing weight, an amazing thing happens. In the Christian tradition we learn that Paul, the inveterate optimist, who founded churches all over Asia Minor before being imprisoned by the Romans, could write from his prison cell, "we do not lose heart" (2 Cor. 4:1). He explains his endurance by attributing his strength to God, writing that "the transcendent power belongs to God and not to us." And in a wonderfully understated way, he admits that "we are perplexed, but not driven to despair" (2 Cor. 4:7).

In today's world, it is often the poet who voices personal despair, feeling what Maxine Kumin calls "her monstrous sense of alienation" in a culture of "polarized hatreds." Admitting that she cannot influence governmental policies, but in order to "live the dream out to the end," she writes, "It is important to act as if bearing witness matters."[1] She and her husband, Viktor, have borne witness throughout their lives as activists for peace and social justice.

Long before Philip Levine won the Pulitzer Prize for poetry, he agonized over his failure to find words "that will make some difference." In his long poem "Silent in America," he describes himself as "Fresno's dumb bard," despairing over his inability to speak "for these and myself / whom I loved and hated." And then in a triumphant borrowing of Walt Whitman's phrase "Vivas for those who have failed," Levine celebrates not only his own despair but that of all others. The poet's words stir our souls, moving us to "the place within me / where I am every / man and woman." His art delivers him from isolation and satisfies his need "to be no / longer only myself."[2]

Such is the power of the human spirit. It would be lifted out of despair. In our human activities, whether through the overwhelming power of another's touch, through their words, their love for us, or simply through the solitary ways of prayer and daily tasks, the spirit will lift.

What force is at the heart of this lifting? A divine activity, the work of our Creator. Now we reaffirm the truth that underlies all faiths: God cares for us. Nothing in heaven or earth can separate us from that eternal care.

 cstasy

"Go wild!" "Get crazy!" Does that sound overstated? Someone urging, "Go for it!" "Go on, dive in! Why are you still just standing there?"

Now hold on a minute, we object. We're standing here, alive and well, because all our lives we've heard and obeyed those cautioning voices, "Look before you leap!" "Calm down!" "Haste makes waste!"

And now you're touting that Frenchman Baudelaire, who urged, "Enivrez-vous!" (get high!), that same Baudelaire known for his debauchery. Here he is, enjoining us to get high on something, whether it's art or poetry or wine. Just get high or (to emphasize the meaning while mixing the altitudes of the metaphors) wallow in it!

In his poem "Danse Russe," the New Jersey doctor William Carlos Williams describes someone doing just that:

> if I in my north room
> dance naked, grotesquely
> before my mirror
> waving my shirt round my head!
> and singing softly to myself:

Ecstasy ~ FGHIJKLMNOPQRSTUVWXYZ~a

> "I am lonely, lonely,
> I was born to be lonely,
> I am best so!"
> If I admire my arms, my face,
> my shoulders, flanks, buttocks,
> against the yellow drawn shades,—
> who shall say I am not
> the happy genius of my household?[1]

What a wonderful image—this highly educated, responsible "grownup" cavorting alone in front of the mirror. It's just such happy geniuses who save us.

Two centuries ago, Baudelaire touted the glories of wine and poetry. Imagine what he would think of modern diversions! They might overwhelm even him.

Each of us knows what it is to "get high," whether the experience is as natural as first standing on a mountain top, or the top of a skyscraper, or as unnatural as drugs. We need to get high, to be moved to higher states. It is those longed-for moments that keep us going through the ordinary days.

"Wait a minute," you may say. "One minute, you're urging us to invite our souls, even learn to enjoy periods of prayerful silence, and the next you're saying, 'Go ahead, get crazy.'" Exactly. Why shouldn't we stretch ourselves in both directions?

We long to escape the dullness of daily routine. In fact, all of us find our own ways to move into heightened states of being, whether in physical intimacy, intense mental focus, emotional excitement, spiritual journeying. We long to be lifted.

And the opportunity to enjoy such states lies all around us. As a Mayo Clinic pamphlet on cardiac care instructed, "Go out your front door. Walk fifteen minutes. Turn around. Come back." My first reaction on reading that was to laugh. After all, anybody can do that. Couldn't we have something a bit more "high-tech," a bit more esoteric?

Then I read the next sentence: "A daily 30-minute walk cuts the risk of heart attack in half." Well, that was old information, but the way they put it finally convinced me. It gave me a great idea, too. Why not go at an unusual time? Early morning would be the best because traffic would be light. Why not put the shoes, socks, sweats, near the bed, set the alarm for five or five-thirty, catch the sunrise? (The only sunrise I normally see is out the bathroom window.)

Here's what I discovered. At that hour my city neighborhood is quiet as a graveyard. Not even the birds are up. But as the light filters through the red oaks, a battalion of wrens, jays, cardinals, doves, even chickadees, come to attention for the day's maneuvers. Now that we stock a bird feeder, whole armies seem to move in. Such chirring, cheeping, cawing, and screeching as they contend for space. Not just squirrels vying for a mouthful, scampering chipmunks too.

Out on the road a few of my heartier neighbors are airing their dogs, nodding pleasantly as they lope or stroll by. Now I am seeing my neighbors in a totally new way. I even know what morning papers they take. When I muster enough energy to speed up my fast walk, I get a thumbs-up from passersby. Granted, these are not mind-blowing experiences, but they are life giving. My mind goes into that different state I remember from downhill skiing, where nothing matters but the steepness of the turn ahead, the rhythm of the turns.

Strenuous exercise, regular physical challenge, competitive sports and games—all those sorts of activities are at least temporarily mind clearing. And beyond mind clearing, they are all actually soul feeding, as are music, dance, writing, painting, actively creating in any form, and finally, at its best, the absolute quiet of standing or sitting still—the joy of silence, into which memory may bring sounds and images, words from other times and other people. At the two physical extremes, from supreme effort to effortless calm, we can be lifted out of ourselves.

Recent translations of centuries-old Arabic and Islamic poems show that their authors reveled in the ecstatic, the cultivation of intense emotion. Robert Bly's translation of Kabir's "To Be a Slave of Intensity" conveys that fervor:

> Friend, hope for the Guest while
> you are alive.
> Jump into experience while you are alive!
> Think . . . and think. . . While you are alive.
> What you call "salvation" belongs to the time
> before death
> If you don't break your ropes while alive,
> do you think
> ghosts will do it after?
>
> . . . .
>
> What is found now is found then.
> If you find nothing now,
> you will simply end up with an apartment in the
> city of death.[2]

If nothing in the world seems to move us deeply, we can try spending some time with young kids—children for whom we have no direct responsibility except to sit and relax. In their quiet moments, they display a huge and enviable talent. They become happily immersed in whatever they are doing, from transferring the same wet sand from one bucket to another, to watching a caterpillar inch its way along their palms. When they are eating, they are all mouth. When they are listening, all ears.

Think of the last time you were so absorbed in what you were doing that you never thought of anything else. Whatever it was that gave you such pleasure, go do that again. Your soul will thank you.

Forgiveness

A recent cartoon in the *New Yorker* shows an office worker replying to a visitor standing in the open door of an elevator. The visitor has asked directions. The office worker points to the number 3 on the office wall and says, "No, this is Avarice. Sloth is on the fifth floor." Is it the antiquated language that makes us smile, or is it the application of the humdrum tone of the workaday world to the problems of the soul?

When we pick up our morning paper, we are greeted with carefully worded, sometimes even sanguine, admissions of guilt by people in high places. Lately, such statements seem to appear on the front page as regularly as the weather forecast. We begin to wonder whether the complexity of our legal system masks the reality of the crime, or whether our moral sense has been buried under an avalanche of plea bargains.

When Edmund Spenser surveyed his fellow Anglicans in the sixteenth century, he seemed to have little difficulty recognizing wrongdoing. To read his long poem *The Faerie Queene* is to be struck anew by his vivid portrayal of the Deadly Sins. And before Spenser, other English writers, like Chaucer and the author of *Piers Plowman*, were famous for their intense portrayals of human iniquity. Here comes the whole unfashionable procession: Ambition, Avarice, Envy, Gluttony, Lechery, Sloth, Pride, Vanity, Wrath, even Despair.

In reality, "sin" is not an "in word" these days. With our many recent advances in the sciences, and particularly with research in the fields of physical, mental, and emotional health, we have a far deeper understanding of human behavior than in the past. We are discovering the complex and interrelated nature of personal and social breakdowns. Fortunately, illness is no longer seen as divine punishment, although the state of our spirit affects all parts of our being.

But these insights, helpful as they are, do not mean that sin, evil, and wrong-doing are no longer real.

As Marjorie Thompson points out in *Soul Feast*,

> Personal and social sin abounds everywhere we look. World powers stand by while despots wreak havoc on their own populations. Ancient hatreds continue to fuel wars all over the globe. Racial and ethnic tensions threaten the cohesion of our communities. Levels of violence and addiction exceed all bounds. Family structures crumble, and children become victims and perpetrators of abuse in their homes and schools. Our way of life places intolerable burdens on the resources of the earth, fouling the very elements we depend on for life.[1]

If we had not thought recently of the ills in the world—of sin, in its various disguises—here is a heart-stopping list!

And what, you may ask, does all this have to do with forgiveness? To forgive, the dictionary says, is "to excuse for a fault or offense, to pardon, to free the offender from consequences." In a legal sense, to forgive a debt means to "absolve from payment." And a further meaning is "to renounce anger or resentment against."

But what if we do not even see ourselves as needing forgiveness, whether granted by our Creator or our neighbor? Do we have to start asking forgiveness for some unknown harm we may have done others? The fact is, as sensitive and caring people, we already know how hard it can be simply to forgive ourselves.

Part of the answer lies in a distinction found in the Episcopal confession. We learn that while human beings may be guilty of "sins of commission"—that is, harmful acts knowingly committed—there are also "sins of omission," those acts we should have undertaken but failed to perform.

Now we see more clearly the accountability implied in Marjorie Thompson's term "social sin."

Until we become sensitive to the needs of others, whether they are as close as family problems or as far reaching as the world's hunger, disease, and poverty, we will not see our "omitted" acts of social responsibility as wrong. The forgiveness we seek on a personal level is clearly tied to the needs of others. We begin to understand the larger impact of working for such reforms as a fair tax structure, affordable housing, "a living wage," antidiscrimination laws. Now the commandment to "love your neighbor" begins to assume a human face, a variety of human faces.

The whole question of sin and forgiveness seems to come down to our intentions, our "state of soul." If we move through the days in a state of soul that is loving toward both our Creator and our neighbor, might we not leave the rest to God?

As a labor leader and imprisoned political dissident, Czeslaw Milosz experienced more personal turmoil and violence than most. Rather than dwelling on the harshness of his life, he takes this realistic view of events:

> Look, see the long shadow cast by the tree;
> And flowers and people throw shadows on the earth:
> What has no shadow has no strength to live.[2]

How naïve to think that our lives do not cast shadows, that we will never make mistakes, hurt ourselves and others, commit dreadful acts we imagine ourselves incapable of. If we are alive, we can and perhaps will do all of that. But we will also rise above every mean act, every falsehood, if we admit them and seek forgiveness. We will be stronger, acknowledging our shadow.

# Gifts

"Oh! I have something for you," a friend exclaims, and immediately we feel a surge of anticipation.

Who doesn't love a gift? Think of your two favorite days: Hanukkah or Christmas or Kwaanza, and your birthday. See? Gifts everywhere. Of course, we have learned the joys of *giving* as well as receiving, but there's no denying that the experience of exchanging gifts is one of the things we enjoy most in life.

Part of the pleasure springs from not knowing what the gift might be. We weigh it in our hand, we test it with our fingers, shake it a little, even smell it. Did it cost a lot? Will it last? Will we love it? And all the while, the giver is grinning happily, watching our reaction, enjoying the suspense. And more often than not, we are deeply moved by the thought that has gone into this simple act.

Now enlarge the setting. Suppose you did not see any package, envelope, or other object that would suggest a gift. Imagine the first morning light, the first moment you wake up. Your mind begins giving you information . . . exactly where you are, on which day of the week, what you may have been dreaming, all that you expect to do. And what has happened? You have been handed the best gift of all. It is your life, given to you, over and over again. Even your rest was freely given. If you had been tired, or even ill, your rest has helped repair the damage.

If life is a gift, what shall we do with it? Is it entirely ours, having passed from others to us? Was it freely given, or are there strings attached? Well, as it turns out, there are some strings. In fact, we find ourselves arguing with the person who insists, "Hey, it's my life!" We argue because we detect rebellious annoyance or immature anger. The words seem to spring from resentment that the speaker should have to consider anyone else.

And conversely, we find ourselves deeply joyful when working or playing with others in a way that finally "takes us out of ourselves," relieved, as the poets say, "of the din of selfhood."

Looking beyond our own lives, we find that in every religion, certain basic commandments are to be followed. Not only are we to respect and honor our Creator, encourage and sustain all life, but also we are directed to discover and use our own unique gifts in fruitful ways.

Stories similar to the New Testament parable of the talents may be found in many faiths. The talent, an ancient and considerable measure of money, carried particular value in an agrarian society where bartering for goods was often more common than the exchange of money. So we sense from the beginning of this story that the three servants have been entrusted with unique objects if significant value, as the master leaves on a journey. We know, too, that the master is a "demanding" man. He will expect something on his return. It is no surprise, then, that when the master demands an accounting, he praises the first servant for his initiative in earning a sizable profit. He commends the second servant in the same way, but severely rebukes the third, who, fearing loss, had buried the talent given him, merely protected it, hiding it from risk of loss.

"What?! Rebuked him?" you might think. "He returned what he was entrusted with!" Ah, yes, but the master wanted more than that. Unfair? Not in the context of all that is freely given us.

Turning to our own lives, we can see a direct parallel. Granted, you may at first find yourself dismissing the claim that we each possess particular gifts. You may have developed the unfortunate habit of seeing yourself as "no one special" or "not really gifted." But your very presence in this world can be seen as a gift. Someone looks to you, looks for you, even if only a neighbor waving from down the street.

Few of us live in that kind of isolation. In fact, most of us move through our day surrounded by others. And to the extent that we refrain from judging or dismissing them, we are creating the gifts of recognition and interest, are learning to see in them the spirit-center.

As we become more in touch with our own spirit-center, we no longer feel ruled by all the things we have to do and make. Think for a moment of the way we describe our lives: we make meals, we make a home, we make a living we make progress, we even make love. But inherently we already *have* all those! If we look at our lives—not from the Horatio Alger, Fortune 500, or even a twenty-first century perspective—from the perspective of "the eye of eternity," we will see a continuously ongoing sacred process of fulfillment. We already *have* all we need, either actually or potentially.

That is why the most exciting thing we can do is to open our spirits to what God intends for us. Not what we think we will achieve, although we have usually come to know what we're "good at," but what will come about through us. And we will not know this immediately . . . not tomorrow or the next day or maybe next month or next year. It takes time because it involves undoing many of the ways we "operate." We *like* being in charge, "making things happen."

The difference is that now, by setting aside our own intentions, noble as they may seem, we are learning how to live within God's intentions. Part of our learning will be discovering what the respected writer, teacher, and activist Parker J. Palmer calls "the ecology of a life."[1]

His term means that each of us has certain God-given talents and limitations. A great part of our spiritual growth rests on honoring them both. As we become more aware of our strengths and limitations, we will be led toward our vocation. We won't build it. We won't choose it. It will choose us. As Palmer tells us, a "vocation is not a goal to be achieved but a gift to be received."[2]

When will we begin to grasp our strengths and our limits, quiet ourselves to recognize the gift?—in our daily periods of reflection and growing self-knowledge. It is then that our souls learn to listen.

And the next time we receive a party invitation and automatically ask, "What can I bring?" we might stop to recall the Big Gift. Our Creator has invited us—all of us—to a sacred feast. We don't need to bring a thing. Just come.

Hospitality

In ancient Greece and Rome, the word "hospitality" carried a much broader meaning than it does today. We know from early classical literature, and especially from Homer's epics, that hospitality then was "a transaction among strangers," as opposed to our modern "transaction among friends,"[1] the Greek root, *xenos*, containing the notion of both guest and host.

When we are expecting guests, we leap to our feet at the sound of the doorbell. In fact, we often begin celebrating even before their arrival, caught up in the excitement of preparation. But let the doorbell ring unexpectedly! Suddenly we brace ourselves, peer out a peephole or a window. How easy it is to welcome those we know. How difficult to welcome the stranger.

In ancient Greece, the laws of hospitality were clear: a guest was to be treated as a brother. Although the stranger at the gate might actually pose a physical threat to those within, he was to be admitted. And in Rome, as early as the fourth century B.C., citizens invited the gods to their celebrations, as in the *lectisternium*, a festival that included food and couches for the pleasure and comfort of the deities. Gift giving and the assurance of safe passage from one place to another were other common marks of hospitality.

But when we turn to our own lives, we immediately sense a vast difference. For many reasons, we have learned "self-distancing," a stance that not only "gives us some space" but protects us from what we fear may be annoying or unreasonable demands. We have been taught to move warily in public places, having been warned by reports of robberies, kidnappings, muggings.

Of course, we are responsible for our own safety. But we are paying a price for our heightened attention. We have become immediately judgmental of strangers. Whether we encounter them in the supermarket or the synagogue, our first reaction is to "size them up," to adjust our behavior accordingly. "Uh-oh, here comes one now!" One what? Derelict? Foreigner? Fresh kid?

I've decided—after catching myself in these quick, unconscious reactions to strangers—to try to stop myself. But it's very difficult! For one thing, I'm pretty sure they are sizing me up—WASP, woman, whatever—and I am trying to make the first move, whether it's a simple nod of the head, a smile, a word.

When an overt greeting is not appropriate, I try to keep a hospitable attitude, an absence of judgment. (Again, it is very humbling to discover how fast the mind wants to pigeonhole every encounter.)

However, this "Stop!" sign on the road of Instant Judgment is proving very liberating. I am finding I can slow down, pause, wait for the traffic to pass, and begin to take in the world around me. It is a remarkably freeing experience, this approach to the world as an invitation.

Finally, let me share this. I was listening to Rudy Giuliani, then mayor of New York City, give his farewell address. St. Patrick's Cathedral was filled with an appreciative audience. As he stepped down from his incredibly challenging responsibilities after the terrorist attacks of 9/11, he commended his staff, the police, firemen, emergency teams, the citizens of New York. Then, at the close of his speech, at a time when some Americans had succumbed to a fear of the foreign or "unknown," he made a remarkable statement. He said, "I want to make something perfectly clear. We in this city welcome immigration. We are a city of immigrants. We welcome immigrants. Let us always remember that."

Isn't that really the mark of our humanity—not how we treat the known and familiar, but how we treat the unknown, unfamiliar?

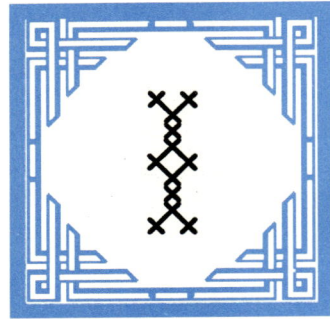# Independence

We come into the world alone. We leave it, alone. Mammals that we are, we will, in infancy, depend entirely on others for long months, even years, to satisfy our needs. Perhaps that dependence is the cradle of our deepest loves. At the very center of our being, most of us know we have been held and nourished over and over. In fact, our ability to be mature, loving human beings is directly tied to the love we have received.

But recall "the terrible two's"—the essential stage when the most docile child shouts, "No!" at everyone. Gradually, the rebel moves on and in varying degrees adjusts to the constraints of family and society.

Looking back after decades, I suspect some of my own self-reliance springs from my father's death three days after I turned eight. He died suddenly, of complications of pneumonia and typhoid fever, just before sulfa or penicillin was available. It seemed impossible. This was the sturdy man who could sweep me to his shoulders, hardly breaking stride, the athlete who carried his racing shell above his head before he set it down gently in the water, recapturing his days as a college crewman.

But if my older sister and I developed a hardy independence growing up, imagine our mother, who became a widow at thirty-two. She had less than a year of college, no money, three small children. Our ensuing years, a colorful saga of our mother's resourcefulness, became a model in our subconscious. She learned to assess whatever was at hand, use it well, keep her own counsel.

Various suitors would appear at our door, often men with money. Mother eyed them in terms of their possible parenting skills, more than by their financial padding. She ended up turning them away.

I remember the night we were sent to bed without supper because we had urged her to marry a wealthy widowed neighbor. He held a seat on the New York Stock Exchange. He also had "a drinking problem" and a temper to match his portfolio. "And why," my mother asked, "should I accept *his* marriage offer?"

"So we could each get a bicycle," my sister and I, aged twelve and thirteen, announced. That was the end of *that* proposal.

Years later, she did marry. Her choice was a wonderful family friend whose wife had died. But Mother never lost her talent for responsible independence. In her nineties, after a successful career as a Girl Scout executive, fundraiser, and editor, she still carefully managed her own affairs. The remarkable fact is that while she was so adept at managing her own life, she had the wisdom to let her children manage theirs.

In her poem "The Journey," Mary Oliver writes,

> One day you finally knew
> what you had to do, and began,
> though the voices around you
> kept shouting
> their bad advice—
> though the whole house
> began to tremble
> and you felt the old tug

> at your ankles.
> "Mend my life!"
> each voice cried.
> But you didn't stop.
> You knew what you had to do,
> though the wind pried
> with its stiff fingers
> at the very foundations. . . .

We can feel all the obstacles the person in the poem faces—the late night, the storm, and darkness. But as that person pushes on, a new voice sounds, his or her own, a voice

> that kept you company
> as you strode deeper and deeper
> into the world,
> determined to do
> the only thing you could do—
> determined to save
> the only life you could save.[1]

This kind of independence, an independence that springs from the soul, has more to do with mind-set than with behaviors. It rests in the kind of "quietness and confidence" the prophet Isaiah described. It is not necessary to "measure up," to become "presentable." The fact is, as the theologian Paul Tillich shows us, we are *already* accepted.

Our independence stems from knowing we have already been embraced by our Creator. No, we're not perfect, nor are we "miserable offenders." We are human beings with a soul, a sacred spirit God has given us. It is that soul, divine in origin, that also assures our unique and independent being.

The poet Naomi Replansky writes,

> I tried to live small.
> I took a narrow bed.
> I held my elbows to my sides.
> I tried to step carefully
> And to think softly
> And to breathe shallowly
> In my portion of air
> And to disturb no one.
>
> Yet see how I spread out and I cannot help it.
> I take to myself more and more, and I take nothing
> That I do not need, but my needs grow like weeds,
> All over and invading. . . .[2]

No one should try to "live small." God wants us to be whole, fully realized. Admittedly, to *be* independent, to speak out, for instance, for what we see is right can be hard, especially if we feel others around us do not agree. Perhaps we are defending someone who has been wronged. Perhaps we are supporting an unpopular viewpoint regarding an issue we have studied, a viewpoint we need to share. Speaking out becomes a form of responsible independence. To exercise that responsibility empowers others to do the same. Independence, then, can be seen not as an isolated attitude but as a necessary part of our concern for others.

**oy**

"Don't touch him!" the nurse commanded as she looked anxiously at the monitor over our son's hospital bed. I could not even touch him? Sure enough, the zigzag line of his blood pressure had spiked just when I placed a gentle hand on his leg.

He was conscious, but very pale, inert, as though all his twenty-year-old life had suddenly been sucked out of him. What *was* this undiagnosed disease? Two days earlier, as we rushed him to the hospital, he was beginning to lose vision in one eye. He had held his head with both hands, trying to quiet the throbbing.

It was two more agonizing days before an excited young woman intern burst into the darkened room where we were sitting beside Eric. "It's a pheo! a pheo!" she exulted. "We know what it is!" And as other staff came in, they explained how they would gradually, painstakingly lower his blood pressure until it was safe to remove the large tumor that had developed on his pancreas.

Where does a pheochromocytoma come from? They don't know. Can it kill you? It can, because even though this tumor proved benign, a tumor of this kind can raise the patient's blood pressure to the stroke level. So the surge of joy we felt at that moment of diagnosis was tempered by the week of cautious waiting before an operation was possible.

Finally, the hematologists decided that Eric's blood pressure had fallen sufficiently to make going after the tumor, which by now was the size of a grapefruit, an acceptable risk. It took more than five hours to remove the growth, delicately and without triggering complications in other parts of Eric's body. Near the operating room, my husband and I sat and prayed for our son and the doctors. We prayed for ourselves, for the other patients, for everything and everyone. We could feel in our very bones how precious and precarious our lives really are.

And then, mercifully, it was over. The doctors were jubilant, having known how great the risks were and how sudden and complete the recovery would be. "Get used to seeing a lot of folks standing by your bed," they told Eric, "because you were pretty far gone, and now you're fine." He *was* fine, too, in such a remarkably short time it seemed impossible he had been suffering for two or three years.

That great upwelling of joy we knew was part relief, part gratitude, part humility. We began to greet each day with new, deeper appreciation. Unfortunately, it often takes such a crisis to jolt us out of constant daily activity into a more thoughtful look at our lives, their direction and final meaning.

When Tillich wrote about "the depth of existence,"[1] he was asking us to look beneath the surface level of our lives, to question the basic assumptions everyone lives by, and instead, to begin to think deeply, feel deeply.

Recalling insights that produced "an earthquake" in contemporary thought, Tillich saw that "an earthquake occurred when Copernicus asked if our sense impressions could be the ground of astronomy, and when Einstein questioned whether there is an absolute point from which the observer could look at the motion of things."[2] Assumptions that had never been questioned were now "blown away." Although cultural and historical worlds apart, Copernicus and Einstein had suddenly shaken the world with their simple questions—questions that irrevocably punctured the assumption that the visible world is just as we imagine it.

And the most overwhelming insight occurred when "the first philosophers questioned what everybody had taken for granted from time immemorial—*being itself.* When they became conscious of the astonishing fact, underlying all facts, that there is something and not nothing, an unsurpassable depth of thought was reached." [3]

Tillich insisted on the need to plumb the depths of our lives, our own spirituality, through greater understanding of our inner and outer catastrophes, through prayer, confession, and contemplation. What will we discover? "The name of this infinite and inexhaustible depth and ground of all being is God. That depth is what the word God means." [4]

Now we confront a paradox. We crave a deeper meaning for our lives, a greater sense of connectedness, a new capacity for joy. But it will be difficult, often painful, to go into "the depths," to be confronted by old fears, unresolved angers, feelings of guilt or shame. It takes great courage to accept the unpleasant truths we may discover about ourselves, our relationships, our beliefs.

Suddenly, we have an inkling of what "pilgrim" means. We are struck with respect for those on "a faith journey." Through the braving of these depths we come to know ourselves as spirit-centered beings. And in that knowledge lies our greatest joy.

*in*

If you have been lucky enough to stand in a hospital room, holding a newborn, you understand kinship. Every one in that room is joined through that baby. They can't take their eyes off the perfect fingers, the sleeping face. They have become the closest of kin.

And even if one of that gathering never had a baby, to be included in such a moment changes one forever. Look at the mother, vibrant after hours of labor, her eyes resting on the pink-capped, swaddled infant as she is lovingly cradled by one after another. Look at the way the new father hangs onto his wife's hand, strokes her arm.

Years ago, babies were born in antiseptic delivery rooms where the mother, strapped into arm restraints and stirrups, was surrounded by masked figures giving her orders: "Breathe! Bear down! Push!" If family were present at all, they were ordered to wait down the hall, with the husband.

Now, in handsomely furnished birthing suites that look more like a hotel than a hospital, the newborn is greeted by a cluster of adoring relatives whose faces reflect awe and devotion. The mother has been encouraged through labor by an exhausted husband convinced he could never perform such a miracle.

In such moments, our kinship glows.

Sometimes we are claimed, drawn close, in the moments surrounding death. But even then, our kin do not leave us. They slough off the body, released from whatever they were suffering, and continue to connect with us in our dreams or come, unbidden, as we continue performing familiar homely tasks. We have all experienced this continuing kinship. As a man mows his grass, the sweet green smell reminds him of his father. A woman kneads bread, and feels her mother standing beside her.

Is it more difficult today to feel kinship with others? Perhaps. Even though we are exposed to an increasing number of people—through the work place, sports, entertainment, television, radio, cell phones, e-mail, and so on—how much connectedness do we actually feel? Our jobs, whether in offices, factories, stores, classrooms, often place us in a work station separated from others. At the end of the day we ride home, often alone, in locked cars to "secure" houses and apartments.

But, as Tillich points out, "We are only in a world [are only alive, meaningful] through a community. . . . And we can discover our souls only through the mirror of those who look at us. There is no depth of life without the common life."[1] Where will we find a "common life" and how will we nurture it?

The most meaningful common life, if we are serious about our spirituality, is in shared worship. That means a group of people—hopefully of differing ages, sexes, vocations, and social contexts—whose common commitment is to their Creator. Some come together daily, some once or twice a week, to express their love for their Creator, to pray, to praise, give thanks, share fellowship, and refresh their bonds with one another. What unites them and inspires them is their innate sacredness, their souls.

When we understand that it is our soul, our own sacred nature, which makes all kinship possible—whether in a church, a community, a family, or the most intimate relationship—everything becomes possible. We will find the "right answers" for our common life. That "finding" may take what has been called "painful self-scrutiny," a greater understanding of our own gifts and limitations. It will involve changing our priorities, our ways of using time and money. We will begin to grasp our Creator's desires for us.

Out of our daily quiet times and our participation in communal worship comes a growing sense of kinship. Things connect. Our inner nature becomes more coherent. We relate more closely and honestly, not only to others but even to the physical world around us. Wendell Berry, the poet, essayist, Kentucky farmer, describes this connection in "The Current," a poem that captures the deeply felt joining of person, place, and history:

> Having once put his hand into the ground,
> seeding there what he hopes will outlast him,
> a man has made a marriage with his place.
> and if he leaves it his flesh will ache to go back.
> . . . he sees the old tribespeople bend
> in the sun, digging with sticks, the forest opening
> to receive their hills of corn, squash, and beans,
> their lodges and graves, and then closing again.
> He is made their descendant, what they left
> in the earth rising into him like a seasonal juice.
>
> The current flowing to him through the earth
> flows past him, and he sees one descended from him,
> a young man who has reached into the ground,
> his hand held in the dark as by a hand.[2]

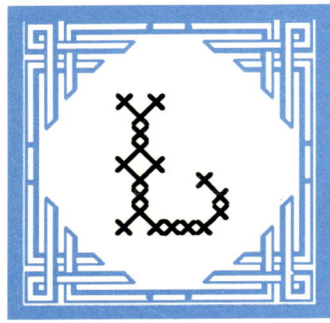

Location

Most of us have never endured prison. But after the 1989 Tiananmen Square massacre, when hundreds of Chinese citizens were killed and more than 10,000 detained or arrested for opposing the repressive government, the Chinese prisons were overflowing.

According to Tina Rosenberg, reporting in *The New York Times* in March 2002, reports of student roundups, false arrests, and prisoner torture appeared in newspapers around the world. Rosenberg recounts the story of a New Jersey-born business man, John Kamm, who was working in Hong Kong as a regional vice president for Occidental Chemical Corporation. Kamm was preparing to appear before Congress to argue that China's human rights record should not interfere with China's receiving Most Favored Nations status, a tariff-lowering measure that would greatly benefit both American and Chinese business.

On the eve of his departure for Washington, Kamm attended a formal banquet in Hong Kong. As high-ranking Chinese government officials praised American businessmen for their expected support in securing the favored status, Kamm had an idea. What if he publicly asked the government representatives for the release of one of the Tiananmen prisoners, Yao Zongzhan, who, according to newspaper reports, was even then being tortured? Kamm did just that. The officials were furious. The banquet ended on a cold, sour note.

However, within a month, Yao Zongzhan was released.

Increasingly, however, other American businessmen backed away from any confrontation with the Chinese government's human rights violations. But Kamm began to notice a connection. If he brought up the names of certain prisoners, within other negotiations, each of these prisoners was released. In a country where it was "always assumed that human rights and corporate profits are mutually exclusive," Kamm, with his long experience with government officials, was able to make inquiries without offense. The officials saw his work as "promoting United States–China understanding."[1] Traveling to provincial capitals and Beijing with lists of prisoners, Kamm has been able, over the years, to secure the release of as many as 250 prisoners.

In 1991 he resigned from Occidental and began his own business devoted to prisoner release. Although his role is not always viewed favorably by U.S. businesses in China, our State Department relies on his expertise. Four times a year he travels to China from San Francisco where he now lives, armed with prisoner lists.

Perhaps such an account seems far removed from our lives. We find it hard to imagine living in a country where hundreds of thousands of people are detained without trial or routinely sentenced to "reeducation through labor" camps. For instance, the Catholic bishop Su Zhimin "has been held informally since October 1997."[2]

The compelling part of this story, "Kamm's List," reminiscent of Shindler's List during the Nazi regime, is its display of one man's moral determination. On the surface, John Kamm was financially and socially located in the best of all worlds, affluent and highly respected. But something in his New Jersey youth, when he was a civil rights activist and a strong admirer of Robert Kennedy and Martin Luther King, Jr., some deeply rooted sense of right and wrong, had a stronger hold on him. When he could not persuade his American business associates to speak out after Tiananmen Square, he began using his own abilities to seek justice, one prisoner at a time. He was morally located.

"Location, location, location." That's the familiar axiom of the real estate trade. No matter how small, old, or neglected a property may be, its value depends on its location. Couldn't we say the same for our souls?

What is it that makes each of us of incredible, eternal value? No matter how apparently small, old, or neglected our souls may be, they have been spiritually located. They spring from holy ground.

Mourning

It comes to all of us at some point. How can we *not* mourn, given our nature? Just as we dance with joy, we will also weep. We mourn what we call "the loss of innocence" in children; we mourn the spoiling of the earth, the mounting wars between religions, between nations.

And closer to home we share the grief of family and friends who experience death and loss. We offer them our support and love, but they are the ones who have to carry on their daily lives, and, hopefully, slowly heal.

Even our rituals to celebrate a loved one's life can heighten the pain. The memorial poems we read, the familiar songs we sing can overpower us with the sense of the person's presence. We open a letter and out falls an early photograph, a childhood letter or drawing, some precious memento that touches our very hearts.

Even our dreams betray us. We waken with a start, realizing our loss anew, asking, "But weren't we just talking to each other? Weren't we just sitting at the kitchen table? Didn't I just watch you open a gift?"

Wendell Berry describes the feelings of a man witnessing the loss of valuable land to the flooding of a river. In "The Slip," he writes,

> The river takes the land, and leaves nothing.
> Where the great slip gave way in the bank
> and an acre disappeared, all human plans
> dissolve.

Then thinking about the loss, Berry writes,

> Human wrong is in the cause, human
> ruin in the effect—but no matter;
> all will be lost, no matter the reason.[1]

Another wise poet, Maxine Kumin, with her husband Viktor, has, like Wendell Berry, also tended a large, working farm for many years. In her poem "Seeing the Bones" Kumin describes how she learned to cope with loss. In this case, the loss is not property, but offspring. Although their daughter is still very much alive, she has removed herself from her family. She is always "off to Africa / or Everest, daughter of the file drawer / citizen of no return." After such long absences, the mother knows it is perfectly right to "give your britches, long outgrown, to the crows" and the daughter's mud-caked boots "to the shrews / for nests if they will have them." These acts are not vengeful, simply realistic.

In the same poem, Kumin describes another defense against loss. "I do the same things day by day. / They steady me against the wrong turn, / the closed-ward babel of anomie." [2]

Of course, there is stability in carrying on the same tasks, picking up where someone else has left off, trying to complete various projects the dead person may have begun. But even in the absence of such routines, we sense another kind of ongoing contact or communion.

Mourning ~ NOPQRSTUVWXYZ~abcdefghijk

Think back. Over the years, those we have loved have always been more than mere physical presences. We always felt their affection, care, and concern for us from miles away. We knew their thoughts. Often, after not hearing from some much-loved person in weeks, the phone rings, and we know intuitively who is on the line. And we know then, at the deepest level, that the beloved's soul is still in touch with ours. We are not invoking some kind of cheap, exploitive séance here; we are simply acknowledging our shared spirituality. Just as we communicate with God, with what Paul Tillich calls "the Ground of Our Being," so we are able to experience that sacred "ongoingness," even in the absence of the physical.

In our daily quiet time we can invite the presence of our loved ones, can share our joys and concerns. Why would we assume they no longer care? Why shouldn't we dedicate our efforts, our work, even our play to those we love, whether they are "dead" or "alive?" The truth is, their spirits hunger to comfort, guide, and inspire us. Our dead *will* "look after us," if we let them.

Turning outward, we begin to learn a new kind of mourning. We move beyond the sense of shock, helplessness, frustration, even anger and guilt. Slowly, as we reach out to others, we are taught ways to lift our grieving into something positive. Other people's illnesses and sorrows take on a new meaning. Keeping quiet company with someone in need becomes a mutual gift. Sitting with a loving child can help. Painting or responding to works of art, playing or listening to music, creating or enjoying a beautiful meal all suddenly have new value.

In "When Death Comes," Mary Oliver describes death as "that cottage of darkness," expressing the hope of stepping through that door "full of curiosity." And because of such an altered view of death, she looks

> upon everything
> as a brotherhood and a sisterhood,,
> and I look upon time as no more than an idea,
> and I consider eternity as another possibility. . . .[3]

We find ourselves drawn closer to others, our brothers and sisters, not only through companionable service but through the gift of communal worship. Hymns, prayers, meditation. How these shared celebrations speak to us when we mourn.

If we turn again to Wendell Berry's poem about the river land lost in the flood, we find the poet describing "the maker moving in the unmade." A change occurs: "The good gift / begins again its descent." And then,

> There is nothing
> to do but learn and wait, return to work
> on what remains. Seed will sprout in the scar.
> Though death is in the healing, it will heal.[4]

Nurture

"Nourishment," the dictionary says, is "that which supports life and growth, promotes vitality." "Eat something nourishing!" your mother chides, looking with disdain at your overabundant pepperoni pizza. All day long we provide our bodies with nourishment, whether it's food, drink, pleasing sights and sounds, or comfortable surroundings.

The word "nurture," however, means something more. The Lain root *nutrire* means "to feed or suckle," and also "to train, educate, and provide continuing care for." Faced with a choice, let us pick long-term nurture over short-term nourishment, for now we are exploring the ongoing strength of our souls.

Have you noticed lately how often we hear the phrase "the spiritual hunger of our times?" Sometimes that hunger manifests itself as a pervasive anxiety, a restlessness that asks, "Is this all there is?" Sometimes the yearning becomes openly spiritual.

And then, whether the insight comes through loss and hardship, or through great joy and gratitude, a growing number of people are brought to an acknowledgment of our Creator. Such recognition occurs when we are brought close to sorrow or death, and to birth and rebirth. Our souls speak to us, affirming we belong to God and to one another.

Those are the special moments, the high points. But what shall we do to sustain those feelings and insights? In the same way that we gratefully sit down, alone or with others, to take nourishment for our bodies, let us withdraw, every day, into a quiet place where we can begin to nurture our souls. Why would we fail to provide a time and space for the most important part of our being?

If we initially feel uncomfortable in this practice, think of it this way. Instead of planning, doing, accomplishing anything during this time, we are trying to let go. We are like a person who has never adventured into calm salt water in the summer. To the novice swimmer, the idea that leaning back, stretching out arms and legs, and simply floating is both safe and pleasurable seems a great challenge to good sense. But it is sane and safe and releasing. The ocean bears us up.

So we arrive at an interesting paradox: We can nourish our hungry souls by actually taking and having less, by releasing. Take nothing into that quiet place except for a certain openness and trust. A stillness. Later, we may experience a sense of detachment, even contentment and joy. And with these, reverence. As Sister Elaine Prevallet, for many years the director of the Loretto retreat center in Kentucky, wrote, "The capacity for reverence comes in proportion to the capacity to let go." She came to know awe, gratitude, and reverence "in proportion as I know where my true security lies, in proportion as I become aware that my life is grounded in God, that my own life comes fresh and newly given at each moment from the hand of God. When I live in that awareness, I know it of all other created reality as well."[1]

Among the things we will let go are the negative emotions we carry within us: anger, guilt, shame, jealousy, disappointment—you name it. How hard it is to let them go! How hard it is to even admit we have them. But go they must.

We so often forget and must, therefore, often remind ourselves and one another of two important truths: These emotions are constant "static on the

Nurture ~ OPQRSTUVWXYZ~abcdefghijklmn

line" when we are trying to listen to and speak with God; and no matter how we phrase it, we cannot be separated from "the Ground of Our Being." Nothing we do, or do not do, can separate us from the love of God.

Accept those overwhelming truths. Feel their nurturing presence. There will be ample time, later on, to translate them into action. For now, let us carry away from our private time and place a quieted and nurtured soul, no longer troubled over yesterday, no longer anxious about tomorrow.

# Overdoing

Jan, my friend who superbly manages a high-level, stressful job, called the other day with a lunch invitation. "Let's go to my friend Isabelle's studio. She has some lovely paintings. Affordable, too. And she has an interesting approach."

Isabelle's work *was* lovely—graceful swirls of color, haunting outlines, evocative. It was hard to choose some samples for gifts. While Jan and I toured the studio, office, and shipping room Isabelle had designed, I tried to guess the secret of her success in running her business. It was probably her businesslike approach to inventory, shipping, supplies, her well-trained help, I thought.

No, the secret of her work, she claimed, was painting upside down. Seating herself on an old revolving piano stool, she grabbed a brush, bent over, and began making long, easy strokes, pretending she was working on a canvas lying on the floor. She swayed a little, rotating slightly to the left, then to the right. She hummed. We watched.

"There!" she said, suddenly straightening, her face flushed. "You see?" We waited. Was this how painters worked?

"You can't stay that way very long," she said. "You can't go back, touching up. As soon as I feel myself getting dizzy. I stop. This way I never overdo it. The painting will be simple."

Overdoing ~ PQRSTUVWXYZ~abcdefghijklmn

With that, she tossed the brush back in the jar, shoved the stool aside, and ushered us out. "Very simple," she tossed over her shoulder.

Later, I puzzled over why I found it so hard to believe Isabelle. The success of her arresting, beautiful art rested on that simple directive, "Don't overdo it!"

Her lesson in simplicity was not the first to challenge me on that subject. Years before, I had taken a class in clay modeling and sculpture. Somewhere in the back of my brain lives a bossy little fussbudget who thrives on old saws like "Haste makes waste" and "Practice makes perfect." In my class I took a perverse pleasure in shaping and reshaping the clay bust of my husband. Whoever thought that I, a novice, could get such a likeness?

Then my teacher came to check my progress. Her despairing cry, "Ohh! You've overworked it!" caught me by surprise. Wasn't getting every hair in place what a portrait was all about?

I soon learned otherwise.

Off we students were sent to something called "gesture class." Stationed around a large circular table on which sat a beautifully proportioned, bikini-clad man, each of us stood, clutching a large pad and a piece of charcoal. Marion, our instructor, held aloft an old-fashioned silver alarm clock.

"When you hear the bell," she commanded, "each of you move one place to the right, take a fresh sheet of paper, look at the model and sketch *only* the basic lines. *No embellishing!* Begin!"

My first impulse was to sketch feverishly. How could I get it right in three minutes? If I started at the top, I couldn't draw the bottom. If I began at the bottom, I never finished the top. This was torture. Clang! Marion's bell sent everyone scurrying to the right. Her voice erupted, "*Look* before you draw! Look for pressures, lines!"

Slowly it began to make sense. In the brief time, I could hope only to detect where the man's weight rested, which muscles were doing the work, which way the back curved.

At the end of the exercise, Marion surveyed our work. "*Now,* you see!" she fairly chortled. "You are beginning to think like sculptors! You are getting at what is underneath! Forget about doodling with the surface. Focus on what is underneath."

Her advice has stood the test of time. When life suddenly confronts me with tasks that seem impossible, or my schedule is a welter of conflicting demands, I remember those two smart women and how they taught me to focus on essentials rather than on perfection.

Another problem we encounter as we try to keep our lives balanced is the notion that every endeavor, whether in our work, our homes, our pastimes, must sparkle with "creativity." The therapist Thomas Moore, in *Care of the Soul,* tells us otherwise:

> . . . if we were to bring our very idea of creativity down to earth it would not have to be reserved for exceptional individuals or identified with brilliance. In ordinary life creativity means making something for the soul out of every experience. Sometimes we can shape experience into meaningfulness playfully and inventively. At other times, simply holding experience in memory and in reflection allows us to incubate and reveal some of its imagination.[1]

What an interesting phrase of Moore's: "making something for the soul." As we go about our daily activities, let us imagine them as small offerings, simple gifts we have intentionally blessed.

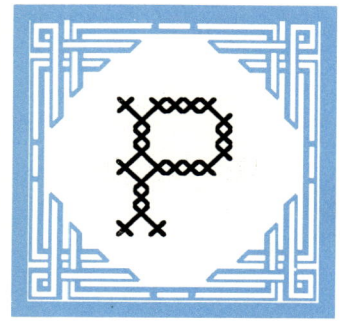

Practices

The dictionary defines practices as "those acts performed habitually in order to acquire or polish a skill." One practice that is followed by disciples of every religion is the deliberate setting aside of quiet intervals during the day. In many monastic orders, daily activities are anchored in regularly scheduled prayer and meditation. The day begins with the tolling of the prayer bell, followed by the observance of matins, nones, lauds, vespers, compline before retiring. Imagine the effect of such a spiritual framework. Every difficulty or hardship could be surrendered to that embracing structure. No longer does the individual have to carry the weight or sadness alone. And in moments of pleasure and joy, what a shared celebration!

But why the emphasis on habit, on the need to do something repeatedly? We all know the answer. After developing certain skills, whether in sports, artistic expression, communication—whatever—everyone has discovered how quickly they evaporate when not used. "Back to square one!" we hear ourselves saying, with annoyance, if our usual routine has been interrupted.

Our souls are no different. In fact, because they have often suffered from neglect, they need even more time to "warm up," "get in shape." Perhaps we have turned toward them so little they jump with surprise at our greeting. But this is the heartening news: They respond like a child catching sight of a loved one. They welcome us. They don't hold grudges.

Now we need to set aside a quiet time, a "window" of stillness. These breaks in our normal routine may begin with a morning affirmation, a period as brief as the time spent scanning the daily paper. They may be scheduled later in the day or after a meal. Short "centering" breaks may occur spontaneously as we wait for a light to change, a phone to be answered. They are the moments when the soul turns toward its Creator, in praise, in thanks, in asking for help or simply in silence, allowing our minds to be still. What an opportunity—ours, freely given.

Well, you say. Here I am. I've found a quiet place. I've even set aside a specific time to be here. Now what? Nothing much seems to be happening. My mind starts gearing up, nagging me to "get up and get going."

Tell it to be quiet. Oh fine, you say, now I have *two* voices in my head. Hold on a moment, now. You didn't learn touch typing in an hour or driving a car in a day. Sit back and practice relaxing. You can start at the toes, as some yoga teachers do, or at the neck and shoulders, where most of our tension resides. Deliberately loosen those muscles that keep you alert to every outside distraction. Take some deep breaths. Perhaps place your hands, palms up, in your lap. You don't have to "hold on" to anything. You are in a safe place.

As you ease into an awareness of things other than yourself, you might try a word or two of thanks, of acknowledgment. Here you are, relatively healthy in mind and body. What a gift. For now, your needs have been pretty well met. You have been granted a high degree of freedom. If you have never allowed yourself to escape the constant reminders of your responsibilities—your job, your family, your partner, your volunteer work, even your hobbies—step outside that stifling mind-set now. They will all be there later, if you want them.

Practices ~ QRSTUVWXYZ~abcdefghijklmnop

For now, you have only yourself in this quiet place. And because you are, in your deepest being, a spiritual creation, allow that spirit to breathe, undisturbed by your mental and physical voices. Just breathe. Your soul doesn't have to speak. Later, it may have all kinds of things to share. Right now, it is learning it's safe simply to be still. More than safe. Welcomed. Appreciated. Embraced.

After a few minutes, you may want to get up, go elsewhere. Before you leave this quiet place, offer a short affirmation and thanks. You might say, "Thank you, God, for this soul within me. Thank you for the blessings of my life. May your spirit lead me and guide me throughout this day." Stand up and stretch. Go about your day knowing you have taken a step in a new direction. No one is expecting you to look or act any differently. No one is going to hand you an evaluation form to complete before you leave. But you have embarked on what will be the most fulfilling journey of your life. You are strengthening your soul.

When you come back to this place tomorrow, repeat the practices that helped you to center yourself, to become quiet and receptive. Notice the word *tomorrow*, not *soon* or *again* but the very next day and then the next. Soon this observance will no longer feel like an assignment. You will find it easier to free your mind of its constant busyness, to center yourself. You are being welcomed into the largest imaginable context, into the whole realm of the spirit, what some theologians have called "the mind of God," others "the Ground of our Being."

And because you have begun honoring, in deliberate and visible ways, the sacredness of your own being, you will understand prayer and meditation differently. You will not see prayer as simply asking. Rather, because you have recognized that you are an essential part of a wonderful, ongoing sacred process, you will want to give thanks and praise.

You will find you can let go of old fears, anxieties, hurts, and angers because you now see yourself and others in a totally different way. You will want to say prayers of thankfulness and confession, just as you will want to pray for others, knowing such intercession is one of the most generous gifts a person can give or receive.

A wonderful thing is going to happen. One day you will discover you did not leave your prayer practice in your quiet place. It came with you during the day. You will hear your spirit, awakened and strengthened, speaking in you. It may be in praise, in thanks, in devotion, or in joy.

The Native American poet Joy Harjo put it this way:

> To pray you open your whole self
> To sky, to earth, to sun, to moon
> To one whole voice that is you.
> And know there is more
> That you can't see, can't hear
> Can't know except in moments
> Steadily growing, and in languages
> That aren't always sound but other
> Circles of motion.[1]

uiet

Imagine, if you can, relishing the sound of a nearby mosquito. Yes, mosquito.

Sitting at sunrise by his open door, Henry Thoreau felt "as much affected by the faint hum of a mosquito making its invisible and unimaginable tour through my apartment at earliest dawn . . . as I could by any trumpet that ever sang of fame . . . there was something cosmical about it; a standing advertisement, till forbidden, of the everlasting vigor and fertility of the world."[1] Think of it: "something cosmical"! What a gift, to see in one of the most commonly despised insects something of universal worth and interest. An "advertisement," a beckoning message about things everlasting.

When Thoreau decided, over 150 years ago, to escape "this chopping sea of civilized life," he set himself up in a simple cabin on Walden Pond. "I went to the woods because I wished to live deliberately, to front only the essential facts of life, and see if I could not learn what it had to teach, and not, when I came to die, discover that I had not lived."[2] In that solitude, surrounded by views of the Massachusetts countryside and the tranquil pond, he also discovered the joys of quietness.

It takes conscious effort to honor our need for quiet. Not only are we deluged by appeals to all our senses, but the fact is that throughout our lives we have been urged to be active, to "get things done, get on with it." We measure worth not by input but by output. So when we finally feel the urge to follow the injunction "Be still, and know that I am God," we are forced to reorder our priorities.

In *Centering, in Pottery, Poetry and the Person*, teacher and artist Mary Caroline Richards offers this view of human nature: "The body of man is a listening chamber; it is a lyre, which reverberates." She goes on, "We play what we hear. Is this not a useful image of man? He plays what he hears. And what he hears plays through him from the impact of the world upon him and from the nature of his instrument. Thus he has the double adventure of knowing himself and of studying the forces that play upon him."[3]

Well, yes, it can be a double adventure, or a double disappointment. In the absence of daily time for quiet, let alone reflection, we certainly are not going to become "a listening chamber," an ear turned toward our souls. Nor will we see more clearly the forces—physical, emotional, mental, and spiritual—that are playing upon us.

In our daily quiet time, we are training ourselves to settle down, center, and become receptive. We deliberately exclude the constant clamor Baron Wormser describes in his "American Poem of the Senior Citizenry." In that poem, a farmwife stands at her kitchen window, musing about her "solitary labor," saying to herself, "This country doesn't know enough to shut up." She goes on, "People fear the land. They gather in cities, and they talk. / Always talking like on the damn TV." Wormser says of her stillness, "She has the quiet keys. / She could be a cat."[4]

We, too, can own "the quiet keys," enjoy the silences of a cat. When we leave our quiet place, we can carry with us the same attentiveness that allows God to

Quiet ~ RSTUVWXYZ~abcdefghijklmnopqrstu

"get through to us." Our lines won't be constantly busy. We will be surprised at the variety of ways God has been waiting to reach us—sometimes through the simple repetition of our everyday activities, sometimes through contact with others, often through joy, certainly through sadness.

If you enjoy a strong visual image, you might smile at the thought of Henry Thoreau (do you suppose he bothered with one of those ancient black wool bathing suits?) plunging at daybreak into Walden Pond. He claimed it was the holiest time of the day, a time when "all memorable events transpire."[5] A time for contemplation and true awakening.

Well, let's take the plunge, waking up to what our Walden friend called "our Genius," our spiritual element, rather than to the world's routines. He saw us freeing ourselves of dull habits, joyfully capable of responding to "our own newly-acquired force and aspirations from within, accompanied by the undulations of celestial music, instead of factory bells. . . ."[6] May it be so!

# Resourcefulness

Who knows better than a farmer how to be resourceful? At the mercy of the seasons and often removed from any neighbors, farmers have always relied on their own ingenuity and frugality. The poet Maxine Kumin often writes of ways she and her husband, Viktor, handle the challenges of running a large New Hampshire farm

For instance, when an old claw-footed bathtub became too awkward for indoor use, it was moved to the fields to serve as a watering trough. They discovered that the extra pages in the Sunday *Times* came in handy for wrapping immature, green tomatoes destined for the root cellar. Kumin even wrote a wonderful poem titled "Excrement," in which she reminds us of the importance of manure. Waste not, want not!

Still, in our market-driven culture, "making-do" or displaying resourcefulness can be a challenge. We consciously have to resist the constant inducements to buy, to own, to "upgrade." When the economy lags, we are urged to spend, as a demonstration of our patriotism. When the economy is strong, we keep on spending, often at the expense of our savings.

Older folks recall a wartime appeal to resourcefulness. It went, "Fix it up, wear it out, make it do, or do without." Nowadays we have little time for repairs or patch-ups. In fact we are enjoined to replace rather than to repair—a broken appliance, an older car, or even, in some cases, a faltering relationship.

But let's enlarge the meaning of *resourceful*. Just as *hopeful* means full of hope, let's make *resourceful* mean full of resources. Stop, those of us who enjoy reasonably good health—physical, mental, and emotional—stop for a moment to take stock. In this technologically advanced world, a growing number of us will lead longer, healthier lives. So, on the surface, we seem to be making good use of many resources.

The resources that go untapped, however, are often spiritual. Does that sound farfetched? Try to recall the last time you consciously put aside your daily activities, constant busyness. Try to recall the last time you gave yourself the gift of silence, the last time you freed your mind of all your surroundings. Perhaps you were briefly still after a funeral or some other deep loss, as you made an effort to put life in a broader perspective. Grief makes us adjust our viewpoint.

But what we are seeking here is not just a changed "take" on life, but a reawakening of our soul's natural resources. Whatever happened to our sense of wonder? Our awe? Our childlike joy in a new day or our once-insatiable curiosity? In fact, the last time we may have asked Why? might have been out of sheer frustration: "*Oh, why?*" actually more an exclamation than a question.

The way to reawaken our soul's resources is clear. In fact, it is not much different from any other plan we undertake; it just takes time and faithfulness. By deliberately setting aside a quiet time each day, a period of meditation, praise, and prayer, we become accustomed to a "spiritual discipline." That term sounds a bit off-putting, but it should not be. These are the moments of "letting go," of allowing ourselves to feel a thankful awareness of our Creator. Our spirits will develop a growing vitality as our quiet times become the anchor-point of the day.

And why should such a result seem unlikely? Think how healthy and "alive" we feel after strenuous exercise, after intense emotional and mental satisfaction. Even strangers remark on the changed expression on our faces, describe it as the "glow of health." We see awakened spirits in the faces of newlyweds and new parents. If our bodies so clearly reflect the way we treat them, how much more our souls!

One of the surest ways to build our soul's resources is to be willing to receive, to develop a receptive attitude. We are not in the habit of receiving, whether in response to some well-meant advice, a sincere compliment, even an unexpected gift. We see ourselves as givers and doers, well equipped to "take the lead," move through life independently.

In her thought-provoking book *The Cup of Our Life*, Joyce Rupp recounts her immediate negative reaction to an unsolicited gift. After being away from home for several weeks, she returned to find "a huge heap of mail." Her irritation grew as she thought of all the time it would take to open letters, sort them, and respond. In the pile, lay an envelope containing a cassette tape. There was no accompanying letter, and she did not recognize the name of the sender. She writes,

> I grouched and grumbled to myself for a day and then decided I had better find out what was on that cassette tape. I discovered that it was sent by a blind woman. It contained one of the most beautiful letters I have ever received. I was deeply humbled and very regretful of my initial response. Here was a gift being given to me that I was ready to reject because I didn't want to take the time to listen to it. I was only willing to pour out a thimblefull of my time and attention for someone else while God was offering me a bushel basket of golden insights and reflections.[1]

Resourcefulness ~ STUVWXYZ~abcdefghijklm

What a disarming confession! Haven't we all, at some time, closed ourselves to a "bushel basket" of unexpected wealth?

As we become accustomed to receiving, yes, welcoming God's presence in our lives, we find answers to questions like those raised by Mary Caroline Richards in *Centering:* "But how are we to love when we are stiff and numb and disinterested? How are we to transform ourselves into limber and soft organisms lying open to the world at the quick? By what process and what agency do we perform the Great Work, transforming lowly materials into gold?"[2]

The answer lies in our joyful acceptance of our sacred nature. In her further defining of love, Richards says, "Love, like its counterpart Death, is a yielding at the center." It reveals itself in "intelligent cooperation, sensitive congeniality, physical warmth. At the center the love must live." By discovering and nurturing our power to love, we are transformed from numb creatures into vibrant beings.

When we think about it, we already know our greatest resource. It is God, who has created and who sustains us. When we accept that truth, we have a new understanding of ourselves. Richards reminds us: "Love is not a doctrine. Peace is not an international agreement. Love and Peace are beings who live as possibilities in us."[3] To honor those possibilities is to be supremely resourceful.

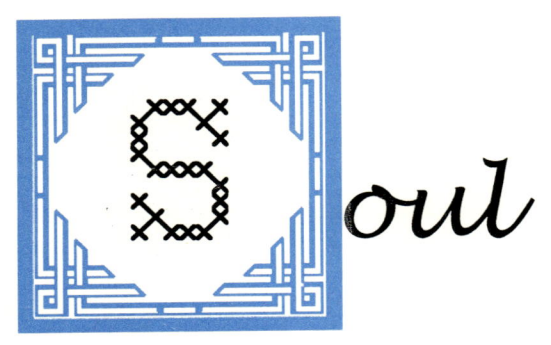

Soul

Even though we have difficulty trying to define it, we all know it's there—that extraordinary "something" that is more than heart, mind, and body. It is extraordinary for its power. The heart tires, the mind weakens, the body fails. The soul endures.

And the soul is extraordinary in its origin. Regardless of the particular religion we embrace (or do not embrace), each of us carries within us that essential spirit given by our creator. Majorie Thompson describes it as "the depth dimension of all that we know as life."[1] Thompson tells us that the soul "is not one slice of existence but leaven for the whole loaf," influencing "every other dimension of our being."[2]

It is interesting that even the most precise contemporary philosophers, when writing about the soul, share the language of mystics and poets. Consider Edward Casey's carefully reasoned discussion of "soul in space": "From the soul's engaging perspective, nothing is out, much less outermost; everything is in . . . and in . . . and in."[3]

Perhaps you doubt that you even *have* a soul. You may feel a deep resistance to the idea that humanity is infused with a transcendent spirit. You will not readily respond to the testimony of the early Hebrews:

Soul ~ TUVWXYZ~abcdefghijklmnopqrstuvwx

> God formed man of the dust of the ground
> and breathed into his nostrils the breath of
> life; and man became a living soul. (Gen. 2:7)

Even so, at least allow yourself to acknowledge the stirrings of empathy you feel at the sight of human suffering. In the same way, recognize the genuine pleasure you take in a friend or loved one's successes or triumphs. What part of your being is moved, regardless of your mind or heart? What is it that responds? It is your soul.

The poet William Blake saw all too clearly the squalor, disease, and corruption of eighteenth-century London, but his writings, paintings, and engravings brim with his certainty of our innate spirituality. Acknowledging the often horrific conditions of his times, he could write, "Joy and woe are woven fine / A clothing for the soul divine."[4]

In ancient times, Plato believed that the soul contained four inner figures: the poet, the priest, the lover, and the prophet. Imagine. Think for a minute of the great number of people who, this very moment, are conscientiously working to develop their bodies—men and women training and straining to sculpt a "six-pack," that corrugated double stack of abdominal muscles to show off at the beach. That's okay. It promotes health. It makes body watching enjoyable. But what if some of that exertion and watching were directed toward all those exciting figures Plato saw in our souls?

Even people who claim to dislike poetry summon their inner poet on special occasions. Is there a birthday? They write a jingle. A roast? They write an insulting poetic parody. They fall in love? They e-mail a love poem.

Whether expressed in the joyful lyric, the stirring anthem, or the somber elegy, in the most intimate and moving hours of our lives we instinctively turn to poetry, music, and song to express our feelings. The poet in our soul is speaking.

When might we think of ourselves as priests? We play that role when we minister to others, whether through small acts of kindness or more elaborate rituals. Parents have a similar experience in certain rites of passage: a child's first tearful trip to the barbershop, the loss of the first "baby" tooth, the sudden pang of seeing a child off on the school bus to kindergarten. Think of the later passages signaled by the deepening of a teenage boy's voice, the first time a girl menstruates, the dreaded driver's-license test. Think of all the preparations (sometimes, overly elaborate) surrounding a marriage or a birth. Our spirits rejoice in ritual. Recall the beauty of celebrations of a life when that life has ended. We watch over all these rituals like the priests of our lives. We watch, we conduct, we bless as best we can.

All of us know the soul harbors a lover. How we nourish her image, yearn for her lovely satisfactions . . . that voluptuous, sweet-smelling lover. In fact, in our present day, the image of the lover in our soul probably gets more attention than any other. From the wiles of Madison Avenue to the liturgy of the church to the advice of the psychotherapist, we are enjoined to love, be loved.

But how complicated our culture can make it. If we never listened to our souls, we would think only diamonds were our best friends, only tall, thin, and blonde were beautiful. Think how far the popular image of beauty is removed from the exciting beauty of Helen Keller, tapping signals into the palm of her teacher, or the bravery of Amelia Erhart, the empathetic saintliness of Simone Weil. In remembering such women, the importance of loving oneself, loving one's dream, suddenly becomes meaningful.

The last figure in Plato's understanding of the soul is that of a prophet, the part of our psyche that carries our deepest hopes and fears, promises and warnings. Rather than thinking of a prophet as some bearded sage given to oracular pronouncements, let us consider for a moment the progress, small though it may be, of some forward-thinking men and women around the world.

In recent decades leaders in a variety of fields—the natural and social sciences, medicine, law, philosophy, and others—have collaborated in what could be called "global prophecy." The conclusions they draw from shared data are not always in agreement, but hope lies in the effort. Worldwide relief and health organizations are better prepared to deal with disasters; humanitarian programs can be internationally based. In such cooperative endeavors, we yearn for prophetic vision.

But turning now to our own wisdom, those things we know for and from ourselves, there is no question we have soul stirrings. We know the "good trembling" of fear, awe, excitement, joy. We are moved to tears by human cruelty and suffering. The deepest bonds of love and friendship spring from our souls. And what does God want for us? To strengthen those stirrings, to bring us into that inner health and integrity for which we were always intended. As Wendell Berry writes in "The Hidden Singer,"

> The gods are less
> for their love of praise.
> Above and below them all
> is a spirit that needs
> nothing but its own
> wholeness.
> Its health and ours.
> It has made all things
> by dividing itself.
> It will be whole again.[5]

 _ime_

"That magic moment," the love song went, "forever will it shine." It may shine, but try as we may to hang on to it, it is gone. It seems that no sooner are we happily caught up in our work (or play) than the timer or the beeper goes off, the doorbell or telephone rings.

The poet Bill Brown wrote in "October Poem,"

> One can stop time only in dreams,
> but at the edge of a season, I sense
> a slowing of the blood; something resolute
> and fleeting is remembered for an hour,
> then forgotten. [1]

The beginning of a new season calls for its own rituals, a way of commemorating the past, honoring the future. Putting up the bird feeder, hauling dead leaves off to the compost heap, unpacking the Christmas ornaments—every simple job carries memories and promise. Brown's poem continues:

Time ~ UVWXYZ~abcdefghijklmnopqrstuvwx

> This morning hope comes in little rituals
> lost to summer: splitting wood, gathering
> kindling from oak branches at the fence.
> Building the first fall fire is like lighting
> a prayer candle to some space lost
> among the daily rhythms of the heart.[2]

It's a wonderful image—that kneeling before the farmhouse hearth striking the match that will bring the kindling to life. Deep in our own memory, we feel all the first fires of other years—October, Thanksgiving, Christmas.

When we free ourselves of the idea that we are working alone, even routine chores or practices assume new meaning. The meals we prepare and share with others, the cleaning up (or what used to be called the "clearing away" when meals were more elaborate), the making of beds, caring for animals, all these routines could, ideally, be conducted as though we were, at every moment, in the presence both of loved ones and of a divine presence. Imagine such a view of our lives—to have "home companions" who are not only loving, forgiving, and patient but eternally interested in our well-being!

There are other ways we can "reinterpret" time, loosening its seeming control over us, by honest work for instance. Although it is hard to invest sheer drudgery with beauty, anyone who has been caught in a meaningless job, having to "put in time," can understand Philip Levine's line "We are the dignified / by dirt." Levine and a fellow laborer were working in the rain, breaking up old Interstate curbing in Michigan. His buddy, groaning under the weight of the wheelbarrow, tells him, "Slow down, man!" But Levine says, "I was into it." He keeps on at a wild pace even though the job is endless, and he knew "we aren't / ever gonna make Monroe."[3] The human spirit finds ways to outwit time and place.

We might ask ourselves why we feel we have so little time. In the first place, consider the irony in the proliferation of time- and labor-saving devices and our seeming lack of any "free time"? Where did all that "saved" time go?

If we could find it, how would we like to spend it? The very word "spend" implies it is gone forever. But if we could "invest" time, where would we find the best return? The fact is, as William Paulsell points out in "Ways of Prayer,"

> It is unlikely that we will deepen our relationship with God in a casual or haphazard manner. There will be a need for some intentional commitment and some reorganization in our own lives. But there is nothing that will enrich our lives more than a deeper and clearer perception of God's presence in the routine of daily living.[4]

"Intentional commitment" and "reorganization." On the one hand, how we shudder at the thought of deliberately rethinking our routines! On the other hand, we are creatures constantly willing to revise our lives if we think the change will make us happier. From the way we eat, dress, exercise, work, play, sleep, to where we live or whom we marry, we willingly try new adventures if convinced of a happy outcome.

Our new commitment to a daily quiet time, a time for our souls, *will* require some reorganizing of time, perhaps even space. And in that dedicated time, we will discover how to let go of our busyness.

We will step "outside time," as we consciously turn our minds toward our Creator, opening ourselves to that surrounding and loving spirit that *is* "the Ground of our Being." Once we recognize and honor our own sacred nature, we see everything differently. Suddenly, we relate to others with totally new under-standing, acknowledging in those around us the same spiritual center we acknowledge in ourselves. Rather than striking us as assignments or duties, the daily opportunities to pray, praise, meditate, study—all these and more—become the richest moments in our day.

# nderstanding

Of course, we all recognize the word. Its various meanings refer to intelligence, comprehension, even compassion. Some of the most common expressions in any language ask or confirm that something has been understood: "*Compris?*" "*Capite?*" or even, "Ya got it?" assure a message is getting through. And the typical responses, if only the nodding of heads or the signaling of a "thumbs up," are ways we show we "understand."

But consider the word used as a noun, as in "They had an understanding," meaning some kind of implicit agreement. Now we are considering something more subtle, less obvious but still important, some kind of accord or compact between two or more parties, an agreement that might never have been put into words or writing but nevertheless is to be observed.

Now suppose that God, from whom all life flows, had not only perfect understanding *of* us but a tacit understanding *with* us. From the Creator's standpoint, the agreement could perhaps go something like this:

Oh, unique and wonderful human beings in whom my spirit is always present, acknowledge that I am the source of life. I have shaped you in your mother's womb, I have watched over you every day, I will sustain you in all good, I will enliven your spirit forever. It is in Me that you live and move and have your being.

When we finally acknowledge, deep in our hearts and souls, that this *is* the relationship between us and our Creator, a tremendous surge of emotion sweeps over us. Everything comes into a new perspective. We look at our lives, our loved ones, ourselves in a wholly new way.

Why wouldn't we feel tremendous awe in the face of such power and love? We experience reverence, humility, thankfulness.—yes, perhaps, initially, even fear—but this is a fear that vanishes in the face of our new understanding. In fact, we suddenly realize that the fears we *used* to have are groundless.

Granted, a great number of people live as though they have little, if any, connection with their God, but once we acknowledge we are in a two-way relationship with our Creator, we are changed. Sustained by the unending love of our Creator, we can live each day with joy and trust. This is what *understand* truly means.

To enlarge that understanding, we need to risk the next, deep plunge. It is not only you and I who stand in this sacred relationship, not only you and I who are soul gifted, but every race, every nationality, every age and gender. Suddenly our deep kinship with all others becomes brilliantly clear. Despite all the surface differences, what unites us is our sacred nature, our souls.

But plunging into this deeper level of understanding, a level that will challenge us both intellectually and emotionally, will not be easy. The unfortunate truth is that we are not accustomed to viewing all people as innately connected. In fact, depending on how far away other people live and how different they look or sound to us, we are almost always inclined to think of them as strangers or "foreigners."

Depending on our schooling and upbringing, we may even have been encouraged to distance ourselves from those considered "different" and to view the unknown as a threat. What a challenge it will be to see ourselves as spiritually connected!

Seeing that connection might be as hard as trying to have a conversation with a stone, which is the situation the Nobelist Wislawa Szymborska describes: "I knock at the stone's front door, / "It's only me, let me come in." But over and over the stone replies, "Go away. . . . Go away. / You can grind us to sand. / We still won't let you in." The speaker continues to knock, begging to be let in. Finally, the answer:

> "You shall not enter," says the stone.
> "You lack the sense of taking part.
> No other sense can make up for
> your missing sense of taking part.
> Even sight heightened to become all-seeing
> will do you no good without a sense
> of taking part."[1]

Ah, smart stone. What is more dangerous than a "missing sense of taking part"? The deepest human trauma is the loss of that sense of connection, of partaking, one of the other.

And what is our greatest human gift? To understand that we are one.

 aluing

Recently the authors of a book about teaching had a great idea. They left the six center pages of their book completely blank and called that section "What's Worth Knowing." The authors knew that none of their theories would really "sink in" unless the readers had decided for themselves what they needed to know. If these prospective teachers could not identify what is of lasting value— the invaluable knowledge or those essential skills they wanted to teach—then maybe they did not really belong in teaching at all.

In fact, when we consider our own education, we recall that skills and knowledge, over time, have proved less important than some wonderful teacher's ability to instill a desire for learning. Think of all the tests we studied for and the wealth of material we have forgotten! But when a teacher found a way to excite us, to encourage our curiosity about some subject, we discovered in ourselves that capacity we all have to become life-long learners, explorers, even pioneers in that field.

The Scottish-born American naturalist John Muir was so overwhelmed by the natural grandeur of Alaska and the Far West, he became a pioneer conservationist, devoting his life to preserving huge areas of our country. From the

Alaskan glacier bearing his name to California's redwood forests to the great canyons like Yosemite, he worked all his life to protect our natural wonders. His many field journals reveal his enduring sense of what was valuable. His biographers say he told people, "I might have been a millionaire. I chose to be a tramp." "Millionaire" has such an alluring ring. Not many people would list their occupation as "tramp."

And if asked to name our most valuable possession, most of us would think of the object we would grab if the house caught fire—our family photo albums, a valuable painting, some treasured heirloom. Or given a bit more time to say what we value most, we might respond, "Oh, my health, of course! What's money if you can't enjoy it?"

In the end, the difference between tramp and millionaire is not really about money. It is about the way each one approaches life.

The tramp that John Muir became was an avid explorer, eager to discover and protect the wild beauty of the natural world. The American millionaire at the turn of the twentieth century was usually an adroit speculator, one who saw our natural resources and the availability of cheap labor as tantalizing ways to amass personal fortunes. The difference between the two contrasting personalities lay precisely in their assessment of the world around them. One saw things to guard; the other often saw things to grab.

What we value above all else proves to be intensely personal. On the surface we appear to share many common beliefs: the sacredness of all human life, the necessity of global peace, the nurture of our planet earth, the sanctity of the family, allegiance to our native country, an equal provision of liberty and justice, devotion to a religious faith, the pursuit of happiness. And so on.

And yet, for every one of our earnest "pledges of allegiance," we can easily find a way to excuse ourselves—from volunteer work in peace-building organizations, jury duty, acceptance of a fair tax plan, a religious commitment, a failing marriage. Probably the only commitment we won't reconsider is to our eager pursuit of happiness.

Sometimes absolution from our promises seems the best course. It is true that there are times when a commitment cannot be honored. As we learn more about the causes and effects of mental and emotional illness, addiction, certain deep-seated traumas, we also learn we may have to make life changes, adapt, forgive ourselves and others for not living up to every promise.

But beneath such difficult changes, what is it we value in our heart of hearts? After we set aside the so-called "virtues," the commendable traits of loyalty, obedience, patience, dependability, and so on, what is it we treasure above all else?

Think of Galileo. Repeatedly sanctioned by ecclesiastical authorities, sent to prison, and eventually forced to live out his days under house arrest for confirming through his own observations and in his own writings the Copernican notion that the sun, not the earth, was at the center of the planets, he allowed the authorities to believe he recanted. But in the end, under his breath, he said what he knew was true. Of the earth's journey around the sun, he muttered, "But still it moves."

Or we remember the young girl in the high school cafeteria in Littleton, Colorado. On that day when two boys attacked their classmates, one of them demanded of her, "Do you believe in God?" She said, "Yes," even though she probably knew it would cost her life.

Or think of the men and women who unhesitatingly entered the infernos of the September 2001 terrorists' attacks. It is clear that our sense of integrity, our need to be authentically and wholly ourselves, outweighs all else. We hunger to "be true."

That spirit puts us on a unique and often solitary path, one that the poet Baron Wormser describes in this way:

The path that goes through fire and ice
Looks neither to the left nor right.
It is the path that honors the energy
That beats in the bowels of living things. . . .
Do not look away, inevitable pilgrim.
Do not forget to honor the energy
That is green and dies and returns
With all the decorous strength of the living.[1]

And "decorous," in the line above, is an interesting word. *Decorum* is more than "conformity to social conventions," but also what the French mean by *proprieté*, behavior that shows ownership, actions revealing one's true nature. What do we value above all else? To be true to the best in us, to be true to our sacred nature.

ord

"Just say the word!" we say when anxious to start some new venture. "What's the good word?" we ask when greeting a friend. The rumormonger begins his report with "Word has it . . . ," and the newscaster winds up his segment with "And that's the latest word from. . . ."

Words, words, everywhere. We are told that the first step in appreciating our deepest emotions is to try to put them into words. But we feel speechless in the face of an *inexpressible* joy, an *unspeakable* dread, or an *unimaginable* horror. How can we get our minds around such overwhelming feelings? Once we can put a name to them, we have a beginning.

We have all read or heard stories of exorcists who claim they drive demons out of the possessed by calling them by name. Such is our belief in the power of the word. In Chinua Achebe's stirring novel *Things Fall Apart*, the Nigerian narrator describes the natives' primitive understandings: "Darkness held a vague terror for these people, even the bravest among them. Children were warned not to whistle at night for fear of evil spirits. Dangerous animals became even more sinister and uncanny in the dark. A snake was never called by its name at night, because it would hear. It was called a string."[1]

The writers of Hebrew scripture described man's yearning to "see God," to "know His name." And the answer comes back to them, cloaked in grandeur and mystery: "I am that I am."

The transcendent power of the word, as captured in sacred writings, is acknowledged by all the world's religions, whether Buddhist, Hindu, Islamic, Jainist, Native American, Greek Orthodox, Roman Catholic, or Protestant. Around the world, sacred writings contain the truths we live by. These spiritual and ethical principles turn out to be much more alike than we might imagine. What do we hear in all faiths? "Love and honor your Creator. Love and honor your neighbor."

In Christian writings, the author of the Book of Hebrews reminded his followers in the eleventh chapter, "The worlds were framed by the word of God." And to underscore his belief in the divinity of Jesus, the author of the Gospel of John wrote, "The Word became flesh and dwelt among us." What did he mean by "the Word"? He meant all that we call our God, the godhead, the Ground of our Being. "In the beginning was the Word, and the Word was with God, and the Word was God."

Centuries earlier, the author of Deuteronomy reminded the Israelites why they had survived their decades of wandering in the wilderness. In a wonderfully concrete reminder of God's care, he tells them, "Your clothing did not wear out upon you, and your foot did not swell, these 40 years." Having been led by cloud and fire, nourished by manna and water, the tribes were to learn the source of their strength. The writer makes it perfectly clear. The reason for their survival and the purpose of their journey was this: "That God might make you know that man does not live by bread alone, but that man lives by everything that proceeds out of the mouth of the Lord" (Deuteronomy 8:3). That, surely, is Word in its most exalted, everlasting meaning.

Word ~ XYZ~abcdefghijklmnopqrstuvwxyz~12

When we return to the language of the twenty-first century, we notice a striking contrast. Although the "digital age" provides us with staggering amounts of information and almost instant contact with all parts of the globe, a strange process has occurred. Sociologists call it "a withering of the magic of language." They claim we have become data collectors, capable of impressive linguistic feats, but that language itself has lost much of its force and magic.

As we set out on our soul quest, we want to regain our respect for the power and uniqueness of words. As the psychologist Jim Hillman writes, "All words have roots, histories, families, gender, offspring. They reach back through centuries to the dead tongues of ancient peoples, and they go on accumulating wealth and shedding outworn baggage as they travel from region to region. They bring blessings . . . and they bring curses."[2]

In regaining our awareness of the power of words, we might follow the advice of the mystic Rumi, who centuries ago invited us to "try to hear the name the Holy One has for things." He makes this distinction between the divine and the human view of existence:

> The Holy One taught him names.
> We name everything according to the number of legs it has:
> The Holy One names it according to what is inside.[3]

Let us become more aware of the way we ourselves name things, more sensitive to the pervasive influence of words. And as we look inward, let us ask a blessing on the words of our mouths and the meditations of our hearts.

Imagine you have been asked to help develop software for learning a new skill. The mastery in view might be as simple as the understanding of decimals or as complex as the command of another language system. Your first job is to come up with the best computer signal for an incorrect response. Obviously, designers of educational software want to keep students involved in learning, even if they make a mistake. The signal must be unambiguous without being abrupt or caustic. What will work best?

On your left, you hear someone arguing that all you need is a briefly worded message similar to those accompanying most forms for e-transactions: "You have not completely filled out this form." This brief message would appear as a pop-up "balloon" or be delivered in a pleasantly reassuring voice, in somewhat the same way your grandmother might ask for help with the supper dishes.

On your right, you hear a strident musical discord. You look over and see the designers have come up with a pulsating black X that completely fills the screen. In fact, the error message is so loud and so visually arresting that it has brought a few people out of their seats.

X ~ YZ~abcdefghijklmnopqrstuvwxyz~123456

Obviously, the answer lies somewhere in between these two extremes. The computer will need to inform the student that the answer is wrong, but it should also be programmed to give suggestions, question procedures, supply encouragement. After all, most of us want to know if we're on the right track but don't want to be publicly humiliated. (Do you remember the day you discovered you could adjust the PC's volume setting? Now we can flounder through new procedures with a tasteful "beep" or in total silence.) Eventually, the "hardliners" and the "mollycoddlers" of the conference arrive at common ground, a fairly non-judgmental response to wrong answers and an invitation to try again.

And certainly, one of the blessings of those computer programs—besides the spell check, the dictionary, thesaurus, and hyperlinks—is the speed of the feedback. Don't you wish the same were true of all our life choices? How comforting it would be to have someone immediately on hand to advise us of our errors or our progress, and then give us a pat on the back.

Our first contact with X came in our early school work. We learned its meaning as a word, an adjective or adverb, and we knew it meant "You gave the wrong answer" or "You spelled it wrong." Once we begin using X as a noun or verb—"Those refugees suffered many wrongs" or "It's a pity how she wronged him"—once someone *else* is involved, the word takes on a much broader meaning.

To wrong someone, the dictionary says, is to treat a person "injuriously or dishonorably, to discredit him or malign him." In this larger context, right *vs.* wrong becomes a moral question. In fact, the very word *ethics*, rather than meaning some ivory tower study of what used to be called "moral philosophy," has now come to mean "a study of specific moral choices to be made by the individual in his relations with others." No ivory tower in sight. To treat others honorably or to wrong them, even by mere indifference—these are intensely personal decisions. They go to the very heart of how we live, making up our value system.

Larger social issues that previously seemed conveniently removed from our daily lives now become our concern, as we see their ethical implications. More sensitive to "the common good," we even begin to fathom what is meant by "a global ethic." What, we must ask ourselves, does it mean to live on a diversely populated, shrinking, and interdependent planet?

Whether in matters of health, economics, politics, or the environment, not one of us will ever again be "an island." Difficult as it may be, we manage to grow in our moral awareness. To live in this awareness is one of the greatest challenges of our time.

As Martin Luther King, Jr., told us decades ago, "All humans are caught in an inescapable network of mutuality, tied in a single garment of destiny. Whatever affects one directly, affects all indirectly. I can never be what I ought to be until you are what you ought to be, and you can never be what you ought to be until I am what I ought to be." What a world of both possibility and mutual responsibility rests in those words . . . "ought to be."

Now our understanding of *wrong* has moved beyond simple errors and wrongful acts to a deeper ethical awareness. We see that it is wrong to deny or ignore our kinship with all others. It is wrong to deny or ignore the sacred source of all life. Albert Schweitzer put it this way: "A man is ethical only when life, as such, is sacred . . . , that of plants and animals as well as that of his fellow man, and when he devotes himself helpfully to all life that is in need of help."[1]

May we learn to be ethical, to wrong no one, no thing.

es

"*Yes, yes, yes!*" Our favorite word. We don't want any of those guarded responses: "Maybe," "We'll see," "Perhaps," "Hope so." What we crave is a pure unqualified "*Yes!*"

It hardly matters whether we are the one hearing or saying the word—the magic works. We feel the thrill of excitement when someone "gives *us* the go-ahead"; we know the surge of inner joy when *we* are the ones granting the wish.

Psychologists love to study body language, all the ways we reveal our thoughts and emotions without saying a word. But you don't need to be a psychologist to see how our bodies behave in a "yes! or "no!" situation. In a fast game of charades, that body language would be a great hint.

When giving or getting a "yes," two people tend to move toward each other, arms open, hands moving freely and generously. Smiles appear, cheers heard. Even without hearing the actual words exchanged, we instantly detect feelings of affirmation, encouragement, gratitude.

How obvious the reverse behavior. When we receive, or *think* we have received, a negative reaction, we automatically stiffen, silence our spontaneity, literally stop and pull back. A "yes" strengthens and affirms; a "no" weakens and denies.

Well, you say, this is all very well and good. Who doesn't seek a "yes!" scenario. But life does not automatically provide them. In fact, for many people each day brings more denial than satisfaction, whether in matters of physical health and safety, job opportunity, political freedom, or the rudiments of food and shelter.

If we begin with our own lives, however, how could we ensure we have more "yes!" situations? So much of our day seems governed by responsibilities, schedules, and routines that we may have lost contact with the whole notion of making choices.

This is a great opportunity to use some of our daily quiet time in a review. Within all the responsibilities of a job, a course of study, a family, a relationship, we want to regain our original feeling of willing choice. There *was* a day when we happily said, "Yes!" to all we are engaged in at some moment.

So a first step is a heightened awareness, both of our selves and our surroundings. Parker Palmer's phrase "the ecology of a life" again proves useful. It takes into consideration our talents and our limitations. As Palmer learned from his own "career" and "vocation" choices, "If we are to live our lives fully and well, we must learn to embrace the opposites, to live in a creative tension between our limits and our potentials."[1]

We cannot move through the day in a joyous, trusting, affirming way if we constantly deny parts of our nature. Nor can we live easily in any relationship or community that, as Palmer puts it, "runs crosswise to the grain of one's soul."[2]

Here we are again, needing to consider our souls! And how wonderful that we are now on friendly terms with our souls, having grown so much better at silencing all those other voices for awhile. Do our souls feel at ease with the lives we are living? And do our lives reflect what we are coming to value most?

Yes ~ Z~abcdefghijklmnopqrstuvwxyz~123456

Palmer, a former sociology professor, learned from his own life journey about the underlying contradictions of "success" in America. He found himself caught in a culture that, as he puts it, believes "economics is more fundamental than spirit, that the flow of cash creates more reality than the flow of visions and ideas."[3] Not just in America do dollars carry more weight than visions.

It was, in part, those contradictions that contributed to his bouts of clinical depression. An outstanding educator and longtime, vital member of a Quaker community, Palmer had to work his way through a staggering darkness of soul. What he gained from that experience was a knowledge "not intellectual and analytical but integrative and of the heart." He learned of "choosing each day things that enliven one's selfhood and resisting things that do not."[4] His is a deeply moving story, one that ends in affirmation. How closely our ability to be affirming depends on knowing our souls.

This is the way the poet Rumi, in his poem "Say Yes Quickly," captures our journey toward wholeness:

> Forget your life. Say *God is great*. Get up.
> You think you know what time it is. It's time to pray.
> You've carved so many little figurines, too many.
> Don't knock on any random door like a beggar.
> Reach your long hand out to another door, beyond where
> you go on the street, the street
> where everyone says, "How are you?"
> and no one says *How aren't you?*
>
> .   .   .   .
>
> If you are here unfaithfully with us,
> you're causing terrible damage.

If you've opened your loving to God's love,
you're helping people you don't know
and have never seen.

Is what I say true? Say *yes* quickly,
if you know, if you've known it
from before the beginning of the universe.[5]

Zone

"Playing in the zone." That's the way athletes describe it—that incredible state where the mind is quiet, the body performs perfectly, and every action seems effortless. Whether it is an individual or a team sport does not matter; the player is literally lifted to a different state. The years of training pay off. The mind, body, and spirit play in harmony.

Musicians and dancers probably play in the zone too, when everything goes as planned. But for the athlete, the experience is wonderful because it is not "scripted" or planned but comes unexpectedly, as a gift. No amount of teeth-grinding, mind-directing determination can make it happen; in fact, the more mind talk, the less often it occurs. Sport psychologists describe it as a form of empowerment, freeing the body to perform instinctively.

There is another way to play in the zone. It has to do with where and how we live. People who regularly minister to the needs of others—nurses, doctors, teachers, pastors, counselors—often have this gift. People who tend the earth often have it. Those responsible for the daily care of animals experience it. It is an overwhelming sense of kinship, of being intimately connected, not only with other people but often with animals, the entire world around them, whether man-made or natural.

While for the athlete this elevated state comes through an internal harmony, others seem to experience "the zone" through external events. Moments of their daily work often put them "in the zone," particularly moments of great stress, pressure, or excitement, moments associated, perhaps, with certain universal events, like birth and death.

In "Sleeping with Animals," the poet Maxine Kumin describes a night watch she kept one April in her New Hampshire barn. Bedded down in her sleeping bag, she lay next to the stall of her "vastly pregnant," "wheezing brood mare . . . ten days past due." She had attended other animal births when she could not help—one foal stillborn, one badly crippled. This time she would be there, ready to do all possible for her beloved animal.

Celebration of human "relatedness" appears in much of our contemporary poetry. The respected Ellen Bryant Voigt called her first book *Claiming Kin,* in recognition of the need to name and honor not just her "blood" relatives but her entire human family. Her work reflects our essential kinship.

In an early collection, *Splitting and Binding,* the poet Pattiann Rogers repeatedly writes of the links shared among all creatures. Celebrating the common elements in humans, animals, and plants in a poem titled "The Family Is All There Is," Rogers begins with the instruction, "Think of those old, enduring connections / found in all flesh." She goes on to remind us,

> Seminal to all kin also is the open
> mouth—in heart urchin and octopus belly,
> in catfish, moonfish, forest lily,
> and rugosa rose, in thirsty magpie,
> wailing cat cub, barker, yodeler,

yawning coati. . . .
Remember the same hair on pygmy
dormouse and yellow-necked caterpillar,
covering red baboon, thistle seed
and willow herb?

Even the whinnying noises of "bay mares and bull frog tadpoles" are echoed in "children playing at shoulder tag / on a summer lawn."[1] What a gift this poet has—the ability to detect, beneath the surface differences, the kinship of all!

Playing in the zone, living in the zone—these are the elevated experiences that give so much joy and meaning to our lives. They make us feel whole, valued, connected, alive. Such feelings stand in sharp contrast to the sense of isolation known by anyone who has been physically or emotionally "displaced." In his "uprootedness," the isolated person feels no connection with others. He has become a "nowhere man" whose life is "going nowhere." Often, the seeds of despair, fanaticism, even terrorism, grow in such soil. What will heal him? His healing will require a rescuing and mending of the spirit more than any other kind of care, for it is his soul that suffers.

When we think again of our own souls, we accept the obvious fact that our lives will not constantly lift us into "the zone." In fact, by definition, a zone is a space set aside, not usually frequented.

But we are becoming more aware of those practices that enrich and enliven us. Our souls are being nurtured by our daily prayer and meditation. We have been enriched through communal worship. Grounded in the knowledge of our unique and sacred nature, we are learning to live simply and trustingly. To be "in the zone" no longer seems impossible.

Such trust and simplicity are echoed in the words of the nineteenth-century Shaker hymn:

'Tis the gift to be simple, 'tis the gift to be free,
'Tis the gift to come down where we ought to be.

A Selection of Prayers and Meditations

I said to the man who stood at the gate of the years, "Give me light, that I may tread safely into the unknown," and he replied, "Go out into the darkness and put your hand into the hand of God. That shall be to you better than light and safer than the known way."

— "The Gate of the Years" (Greeting card, Washington Cathedral, Washington, D.C.)

If our spiritual journey begins with our search for the clearing in the forest, what are the instructions for lighting the fire? Even before we light the fire, we must chop down the trees and gather the wood. But as the Kotzker Rebbe pointed out, "sharpening the axe is as important as cutting the tree." Therefore, we must sharpen out own axes and start with our individual spiritual preparations for prayer.

— David S. Ariel, *Spiritual Judaism: Restoring Heart and Soul to Jewish Life*

Let us examine our lives in the presence of God, humbly confessing our sins and opening our hearts so that we do not deceive even ourselves and exclude ourselves from your presence.

— Selva Lehman, Call to Confession #833, The New Century Hymnal

So, OK, I am willing, and I can't do this by myself. I really want You to open me to the beings of light, the souls that came before me and those that will yet come. I want You to open me to the process of revelation, enlightenment, holy spirit, the means You use to bring to us what we need in order to serve You, Life of Life.

> — Reb Zalman Schachter-Shalomi, Preface to "The Prayer of Assiyah"

Make a joyful noise to the Lord,
 all the lands!
Serve the Lord with gladness!
Come into his presence with singing!
For the Lord is good;
His steadfast love endures for ever,
 and his faithfulness to all generations.
> — Psalm 100

Here let me give what I understand to be the spiritual sense of the Lord's Prayer:
Our Father, which art in heaven,
(Our Father-Mother God, all-harmonious)
Hallowed be thy name,
(Adorable One,)
Thy kingdom come,
(Thy kingdom is come; Thou art ever-present.)
Thy will be done,
(Enable us to know,—as in heaven, so on earth—God is omnipotent, supreme.)
> —Mary Baker Eddy

Little can be expected of that day, if it can be called a day, to which we are not awakened by our Genius [the classical term for a guardian spirit] but by the mechanical nudgings of some servitor, are not awakened by our own newly-acquired force and aspirations from within, accompanied by the undulations of celestial music, instead of factory bells, and a fragrance filling the air—to a higher life than we fell asleep from; and thus the darkness bears its fruit, and proves itself to be good no less than the light. That man who does not believe that each day contains an earlier, more sacred, and auroral hour than he has yet profaned, has despaired of life...

— Henry David Thoreau, *Walden*

O Lord, grant that I meet all that this coming day brings me with spiritual tranquillity. Grant that I may fully surrender myself to Thy holy Will.

At every hour of this day, direct and support me in all things. Whatsoever news may reach me in the course of the day, teach me to accept it with a calm soul and the firm conviction that all is subject to Thy holy Will.

Direct my thoughts and feelings in all my words and action. In all unexpected occurrences, do not let me forget that all is sent from Thee.

Grant that I may deal straightforwardly and wisely with every member of my family, neither embarrassing nor saddening anyone.

O Lord, grant me the strength to endure the fatigue of the coming day and all the events that take place during it. Direct my will, and teach me to pray, to believe, to hope, to be patient, to forgive, and to love. Amen.

—Nineteenth-century Russian prayer from the Optima Monastery

Take my life and let it be
Consecrated, God, to thee.

Take my moments and my days;
Let them flow in ceaseless praise.

Take my hands and let them move
At the impulse of thy love.
Take my feet, and let them be
Swift and beautiful for thee.
    —Frances Ridley Havergal (1836–1879), "Take My Life and Let It Be"

I can complicate a very simple and orderly environment. The real source of the complications, the anxiety, the tensions, the guilt, lies within. . . . if we center down and bring our program, with a spirit of detachment and openness, into the presence of God, it is re-evaluated for us: what we must do becomes clear, and some of what we thought we needed to do becomes insignificant. . . .
    —Elaine Prevallet, Sisters of Loretto, "Reflections on Simplicity"

Ho, everyone who thirsts,
        come to the waters;
and he who has no money,
        come, buy and eat!
Come, buy wine and milk
        without money and without price.
Why do you spend your money
        for that which is not bread,
    And your labor for that which
        does not satisfy?

Hearken diligently to me, and eat
     what is good,
  and delight yourselves in fatness.
Incline your ear, and come to me;
  hear, that your soul may live...
       —Isaiah 55:1–3

Truthful Spirit, dwell with me,
I myself would truthful be;
And with wisdom kind and clear
Let your life in mine appear;
And with actions brotherly
Speak my God's sincerity.
    —Rev. Thomas Toke Lynch, "Truthful Spirit, Dwell with Me," 1855

Bless the Lord, O my soul;
and all that is within me, bless his holy name!
Bless the Lord, O my soul,
and forget not all his benefits,
who forgives all your iniquity,
who heals all your diseases,
who redeems your life from the Pit,
who crowns you with steadfast love and mercy,
who satisfies you with good as long as you live,
so that your youth is renewed like the eagle's.
    —Psalm 103:1–5

For what seems an eternity
I have climbed the cloud-tangled mountain

of my life. But here, halfway,
the summit is a vanishing point,

distant and unconquerable,
so I huddle on this jagged ledge,

helpless and too frightened to move,
waiting for the inevitable cold

to slide down the steep and register
bone deep in the gray marrow of my soul.

My dying prayer—
likely abandoned on too thin air—

that someday I will be found
blue and rigid, staring at stars

high above a condemning world
from which I have finally been pardoned.
   —John Smelcer, "Ascension"

Prayer is a heart-to-heart conversation with the divine within. We pray at times
of powerful pain and distress, pouring out our broken hearts in search of com-

fort and healing. We empty the broken vessel of our heart before we can fill it with the healing light of God. But we also pray in small, unconscious ways every time we are filled with the pleasure, wonder, and awareness of everything around us that we too often take for granted. Every moment of awareness of the divine within the world is a prayer waiting to be shaped into words.

    —David S. Ariel, "Why We Pray"

I am the blossom pressed in a book
and found again after 200 years...

I am the maker, the lover, and the keeper...

When the young girl who starves
sits down to a table
she will sits beside me...

I am food on the prisoner's plate...

I am water rushing to the wellhead,
filling the pitcher until it spills...

I am the one whose love
overcomes you, already with you
when you think to call my name...

    —Jane Kenyon, "Briefly It Enters, and Briefly Speaks"

Finally, beloved, whatever is true, whatever is honorable, whatever is just, whatever is pure, whatever is pleasing, whatever is commendable, if there is any excellence and if there is anything worthy of praise, think on these things.

—Philippians 4:8

The Lord bless you and keep you. The Lord make his face shine upon you and be gracious unto you. The Lord lift up his countenance upon you, and give you peace.

—The Northfield Benediction

Notes on Sources

Awe

1. Jeffrey Skinner, "Problems," *A Guide to Forgetting* (St. Paul: Graywolf, 1988), 16.

2. Rainer Maria Rilke, "A Walk," trans. Robert Bly, in *The Rag and Bone Shop of the Heart: Poems for Men*, ed. Robert Bly, James Hillman, and Michael Meade (New York: HarperCollins, 1992), 438.

3. Thomas Berry, "Pluralism and Oppression: Theology in a World Perspective," in *Annual Volume #34*, ed. Paul Knitter (Chestnut Hill, Mass.: Boston College, College Theology Society, 99.

4. Harold Freer and Francis Hall, *Two or Three Together* (New York: Harpers, 1954), 149.

Becoming

1. James Hillman, *The Force of Character of the Lasting Life* (New York: Random House, 1999), 32.

Community

1. Thomas Pizer, "The Seeds Project," Irby Simpkins Informational Brochure (Nashville: Brownlee O. Currey Foundation, n.d.).

2. Ellen Bell, "Everyman," used by permission of Gus and Norma Bell.

3. Carl Sandburg, quoted in *The Family of Man* (New York: Maco Magazine Corporation for the Museum of Modern Art, n.d.), foreword.

Despair

1. Maxine Kumin, "Seeing the Bones," in *Maxine Kumin: Selected Poems, 1960–1990* (New York: W. W. Norton, 1997).

2. Philip Levine, "Silent in America," in *New Selected Poems* (New York: Knopf, 1994).

Ecstasy

1. William Carlos Williams, "Danse Russe," in *The Collected Poems of William Carlos Williams: 1909-1939*, vol. 1 (New York: New Directions, 1938).

2. Kabir, "To Be a Slave of Intensity," trans. Robert Bly, in *The Rag and Bone Shop of the Heart: Poems for Men*, ed. Robert Bly, James Hillman, and Michael Meade (New York: HarperCollins, 1992).

Forgiving

1. Marjorie J. Thompson, *Soul Feast* (Louisville: Westminster John Knox Press, 1995), 79.

2. Czeslaw Milosz, "Faith," in *The Rag and Bone Shop of the Heart: Poems for Men*, ed. Robert Bly, James Hillman, and Michael Meade (New York: HarperCollins, 1992), 275.

Gifts

1. Parker J. Palmer, *Let Your Life Speak: Listening for the Voice of Vocation* (San Francisco: Jossey-Bass Inc, Publishers: 2000), 44.

2. Ibid., dust-jacket end flap.

Hospitality

1. Susan Ford Wiltshire, *Public and Private in Vergil's Aeneid*, University of Massachusetts Press, 1989, 83.

Independence

1. Mary Oliver, "The Journey," in *Dream Work* (New York: Atlantic Monthly Press, 1986).

2. Naomi Replansky, "Housing Shortage," in *The Dangerous World: New and Selected Poems, 1934–1994* (Chicago: Another Chicago Press, 1994).

Joy

1. Paul Tillich, *The Shaking of the Foundations* (New York: Scribner's, 1948), 52.

2. Ibid., 54.

3. Ibid.

4. Ibid., 57.

Kin

1. Paul Tillich, *The Shaking of the Foundations* (New York: Scribner's, 1948), 57.

2. Wendelll Berry, "The Current," in *The Selected Poems of Wendell Berry* (Washington, D.C.: Counterpoint, 1989).

Location

1. Tina Rosenberg, "Kamm's List," *New York Times Magazine*, March 3, 2002, 58ff.

2. Ibid., 62.

Mourning

1. Wendell Berry, "The Slip," in *The Selected Poems of Wendell Berry* (Washington, D.C.: Counterpoint, 1989).

2. Maxine Kumin, "Seeing the Bones," in *Maxine Kumin: Selected Poems, 1960–1990* (New York: W. W. Norton, 1989).

3. Mary Oliver, "When Death Comes," in *New and Selected Poems* (Boston: Beacon Press, 1992).

4. Wendell Berry, "The Slip."

Nurture

1. Elaine Prevallet, S.L., *Reflections on Simplicity*, Pendle Hill Pamphlet 244, Pendle Hill Publications, 1987, 22.

Overdoing

1. Thomas Moore, *Care of the Soul* (New York: HarperCollins, 1992), 198.

Practices

1. Joy Harjo, "Prayer," *The Woman That Fell from the Sky* (New York: W. W. Norton, 1994).

Quiet

1. Henry David Thoreau, "Walden," *The American Tradition in Literature*, W.W. Norton, 1974), 1,278.

2. Ibid., I,279.

3. Mary Caroline Richards, *Centering in Pottery, Poetry, and the Person* (Wesleyan University Press, 1954), 117.

4. Baron Wormser, "American Poem of the Senior Citizenry," in *When* (Louisville: Sarabande Books, 1997).

5. Thoreau, I,279

6. Ibid.

Resourcefulness

I. Joyce Rupp, *The Cup of Our Life* (Notre Dame, Ind.: Ave Maria Press, 2002), 123–24.

2. Mary Caroline Richards, *Centering in Pottery, Poetry, and the Person* (Wesleyan University Press, 1954), 138.

3. Ibid., 140.

Soul

I. Marjorie J. Thompson, *Soul Feast* (Louisville: Westminster John Knox Press, 1995), 15.

2. Ibid.

3. Edward S. Casey, *Spirit and Soul* (Dallas: Spring Publications, 1991), 301.

4. William Blake, "The Book of Thel," l. 53.

5. Wendell Berry, "The Hidden Singer," in *The Selected Poems of Wendell Berry* (Washington, D.C.: Counterpoint, 1989).

Time

I. Bill Brown, "October Poem," in *The Gods of Little Pleasures* (Abingdon, Ky.: Sow's Ear, 2001), 45.

2. Ibid.

3. Philip Levine, "Making It New," in *New Selected Poems* (New York: Knopf, 1994).

4. William O. Paulsell, "Ways of Prayer: Designing a Personal Rule of Life," *Weavings* 2, no. 5 (November–December 1987): 44.

Understanding

I. Wislawa Szymborska, "Conversation with a Stone," in *View with a Grain of Sand* (New York: Harcourt Brace & Co., 1993).

Valuing

1. Baron Wormser, *Atoms, Soul Music and Other Poems* (Latham, N.Y.: British American Publishing: Paris Review Editions, 1989), 40.

Word

1. Chinua Achebe, *Things Fall Apart* (New York: Random House, 1959), 9.

2. James Hillman, *The Rag and Bone Shop of the Heart: Poems for Men*, ed. Robert Bly, James Hillman, and Michael Meade (New York: HarperCollins, 1992), 157.

3. Rumi, "Names," in *Rag and Bone Shop of the Heart,* trans. Robert Bly, 376.

X

1. Albert Schweitzer, *Out of My Life and Thought: An Autobiography*, trans. C. T. Campion (New York: Henry Holt, 1949), 158.

Yes!

1. Parker J. Palmer, *Let Your Life Speak: Listening to the Voice of Vocation* (San Francisco: Jossey-Bass, 2000), 55.

2. Ibid., 41.

3. Ibid., 76.

4. Ibid., 60.

5. Rumi, "Say Yes Quickly," trans. Coleman Barks and John Moyne, in *The Rag and Bone Shop of the Heart: Poems for Men*, ed. Robert Bly, James Hillman, and Michael Meade (New York: HarperCollins, 1992), 438.

Zone

1. Pattiann Rogers, "The Family Is All There Is," in *Splitting and Binding* (Middletown, Conn.: Wesleyan University Press, 1992).

Pages for Reader's Notes

SOUL SAMPLER

Elizabeth Hahn's work has appeared in journals in the United States, Canada, and Great Britain. Two poetry chapbooks, *Out of Plumb* and *Kindred*, were followed by a collection of boating anecdotes, *Hustled Aboard*. She is co-translator with Brenda Casey of *lueur sur la montagne*, poems by the Quebec poet Pierre Morency. A professor emerita of English at Southern Connecticut State University, she lives in Nashville, Tennessee, with her husband. Her activities there include serving on the board of directors of Filmhouse, their son's film production company, and on the editorial board of the *Cumberland Poetry Review*.